New Bru

MW01045871

The New Brunswick Military Heritage Series, Volume 16

New Brunswick
and the Navy
Four Hundred Years

Marc Milner and Glenn Leonard

GOOSE LANE EDITIONS and
THE NEW BRUNSWICK MILITARY HERITAGE PROJECT

Copyright © 2010 by Marc Milner and Glenn Leonard.

All rights reserved. No part of this work may be reproduced or used in any form or by any means, electronic or mechanical, including photocopying, recording, or any retrieval system, without the prior written permission of the publisher or a licence from the Canadian Copyright Licensing Agency (Access Copyright). To contact Access Copyright, visit www.accesscopyright.ca or call 1-800-893-5777.

Edited by Brent Wilson and Barry A. Norris.
Front cover illustrations by John Horton (upper) and Irwin John Bevan (lower).
Spine photograph from www.sxc.hu.
Back cover illustration from http://www.saintjohn.nbcc.ca/heritage/rcn/ship_building.htm.
Cover and interior page design by Jaye Haworth.
Art direction by Julie Scriver.
Printed in Canada on paper that is FSC certified.
10 9 8 7 6 5 4 3 2 1

Library and Archives Canada Cataloguing in Publication

Milner, Marc
    New Brunswick and the navy: four hundred years / Marc Milner, Glenn Leonard.

(New Brunswick military heritage series; 16)
Includes bibliographical references and index.
ISBN 978-0-86492-632-6

1. New Brunswick—History, Naval. I. Leonard, Glenn, 1962- II. Title.
III. Series: New Brunswick military heritage series; 16

FC2470.N3M54 2010   971.5'1   C2010-903102-4

Goose Lane Editions acknowledges the financial support of the Canada Council for the Arts, the Government of Canada through the Book Publishing Industry Development Program (BPIDP), and the New Brunswick Department of Wellness, Culture and Sport for its publishing activities.

Goose Lane Editions
Suite 330, 500 Beaverbrook Court
Fredericton, New Brunswick
CANADA E3B 5X4
www.gooselane.com

New Brunswick Military Heritage Project
The Brigadier Milton F. Gregg, VC,
Centre for the Study of War and Society
University of New Brunswick
PO Box 4400
Fredericton, New Brunswick
CANADA E3B 5A3
www.unb.ca/nbmhp

Mixed Sources
Product group from well-managed forests,
controlled sources and recycled wood or fiber
www.fsc.org Cert no. SW-COC-000952
© 1996 Forest Stewardship Council
FSC

Dedicated to the Canadian Navy
in Honour of Its Centennial

Contents

Introduction

On July 26, 1881, H.M.S. *Charybdis* cast anchor in the harbour at Saint John, New Brunswick. The warship, just acquired by the young Dominion of Canada, represented the first attempt to establish a Canadian navy. Her presence in that bustling Maritime city was no accident. In the late nineteenth century, Saint John was Canada's premier east coast port, one of its busiest commercial ports, and the only major one ice-free year-round. *Charybdis* might have gone to Halifax, where there already was a naval base, but that establishment belonged to the Imperial navy. Saint John seemed the logical place to found a new Dominion naval service. But by the time Canada tried again, in 1910, the Royal Navy was gone from Halifax, and Canada's permanent naval service would be founded there, not in Saint John.

Over the past century historians have traced the roots of Canada's navy through the legacy of the former Imperial base in Halifax—the "Warden of the North," as it was once known. Through two world wars and a long Cold War, much of the Canadian navy's history was made in the broad ocean far from New Brunswick's sheltered shoreline.

But New Brunswick's role in Canadian naval history is greater than one might suppose. Canada's navy calls Halifax its home, but most of the fleet's key vessels in the navy's centennial year were built in New Brunswick. So, too, was Canada's National Naval Memorial, H.M.C.S. *Sackville*: the iconic warship of Canada's formative naval experience in the Battle of the Atlantic. She is the last of nearly three hundred corvettes hastily built around the world for auxiliary duty in the Second World War and the vessel that made Allied victory in Europe in 1945 possible. Preserved in Halifax, she is the monument to those who fought in the greatest war at sea and a symbol of the nation's decisive contribution to victory. She is even named for a New Brunswick town.

New Brunswick can boast a number of other singular accomplishments in the annals of Canadian naval history: from the first naval war in Canadian history in the 1640s; to the little-known Battle of the Restigouche in 1759; to native son Caleb Seeley, who became one of Canada's most successful privateers in the War of 1812; to Sir George Foster, the New Brunswicker whose resolution in Parliament on March 29, 1909, led to the *Naval Service Act* of 1910; to the founding in 1944 of the Canadian navy's first oceanographic research station. Amid all this, New Brunswick also made its own largely neglected and little-known naval history. The province's land frontier might have been largely quiet during the War of 1812, but New Brunswickers established their own navy and fought a relentless small ship war in the Bay of Fundy and Gulf of Maine for years. In the twentieth century, New Brunswick raised naval reservists and operated Canada's busiest defended commercial port and the British Empire's largest dry dock, while the navy's ships carried provincial place names to war and made some remarkable history. The century culminated in the building of the Canadian Patrol Frigates that form the core of the contemporary Canadian navy's combat power. This is the story of New Brunswick and the navy.

Chapter One

Early Days

New Brunswick is bounded on three sides by the sea, with excellent harbours and, generally, an accessible shoreline and navigable rivers. It is not surprising, then, that much of its recorded history involves the sea and ships. Indeed, it is now accepted among specialists that the eastern shore of the province is the fabled Vynland of the Norse Sagas. Iceland's "Saga Museum" displays a map showing the site of Leif Erickson's tenth-century explorations as Miramichi Bay, and it is believed that a sod house—comparable to that discovered at L'Anse aux Meadows, Newfoundland—was established there. This temporary Norse intrusion speaks to the nature of New Brunswick's maritime and naval history: echoes of larger events washing ashore when and where occasion allowed.

Although permanent settlement of New Brunswick by Europeans did not occur until the seventeenth century, European fishermen began exploiting the area in the sixteenth century. By the time Samuel de Champlain arrived in 1603, local Aboriginals were already sailing the Bay of Fundy in small, open, European-designed chaloups and were equipped with steel weapons of European manufacture. Champlain's voyage of exploration took him down the Atlantic coast from the St. Croix River to the Saco River, accompanied by both a Mi'kmaq and a Maliseet chief, each sailing in his own vessel. Once south of the Saco, Champlain discovered a sedentary agricultural people who still worked with stone tools. As historian Tony Kennedy has observed, "By adopting European coastal vessels and styles of navigation, the Mi'kmaq and Maliseet had become regional middlemen, transporting furs from the Gulf of Maine to more profitable markets in the Gulf of St. Lawrence. They made extensive use of European ships and weapons to enforce their interests within the region."

It was, therefore, the transfer of technology by Basque whalers and fishermen harvesting the resources of the Gulf of St. Lawrence that prompted the first recorded maritime war in Canadian history. The origins of the Tarrentine War, fought by the Aboriginal people of the area between 1603 and 1619, lay in the struggle to control access to this new technology and the desire to avenge the killing of some prominent Mi'kmaq and Maliseet chiefs. In 1603, open warfare erupted between a confederacy of these two tribes led by the Mi'kmaq chief Membertou and their rivals in southern Maine and New Hampshire led by the Penobscot chief Bessabes. Membertou's confederacy was armed, in author Dr. Olive Dickason's words, "with swords, cutlass, and even muskets," as well as steel arrowheads and knives. While raids occurred overland and along river systems, the Mi'kmaq-Maliseet confederacy also used 12-ton, forty-foot-long chaloups as troop transports and supply ships. One Jesuit account commented that they handled them "as skilfully as our courageous and active sailors in France."

Much of the impetus for the war subsided when Membertou died in 1611 and Bessabes was killed four years later. Epidemic diseases brought by Europeans also struck Aboriginal communities hard, and by about 1619 the Mi'kmaq-Maliseet alliance had gradually dissolved. Mi'kmaq raiding parties, however, continued to strike as far south as Massachusetts until the 1630s.

The Tarrentine War and the high incidence of Aboriginal mortality from disease — estimated at over ninety percent among some communities along the northeast Atlantic coast — coincided with a European struggle for control of the maritime region of Canada. Ironically, it began not between rival nations but among the French, the first Europeans to settle the area permanently. In the sixteenth century, European monarchs extended their empires by granting commercial charters to private individuals or groups whose loosely regulated activities often led to private wars in distant lands. Such was the so-called Acadian Civil War.

In 1632, Charles de Saint-Étienne de La Tour, son of the seigneur of Port-Royal (in what is now Nova Scotia), built a fortified trading post at the mouth of the St. John River. During its short twenty-two-year history, what became known as Fort La Tour was besieged five times and changed hands among French, Scottish, and English adventurers and privateers. During the 1640s, in particular, Charles La Tour and his rival from across the Bay of Fundy, Charles de Menou d'Aulnay, fought for control of Acadia. Both men commanded small private armies and fleets of ships that linked their New World possessions to Europe. Their conflicting interests overlapped, however, and in 1641 their fleets fought an indecisive battle off Port-Royal. D'Aulnay then arranged to have La Tour ordered back to France; in 1642, La Tour's having failed to go, d'Aulnay was ordered to arrest him. Hearing the news, La Tour sent his wife Jacqueline to France to plead his case; d'Aulnay, meanwhile, blockaded Saint John harbour. When Jacqueline returned aboard a supply ship, having successfully defended her husband's case, she and Charles escaped to Boston. There, they raised a force of mercenaries and returned to Saint John with four ships, drove off d'Aulnay's blockade, chased his fleet across the Bay of Fundy, and burned the mill at Port-Royal.

An uneasy standoff persisted for a couple of years while both d'Aulnay and Madame La Tour made their claims once again in Paris. This time d'Aulnay won. In February 1645, while Charles was away in Boston, d'Aulnay brought his ship, the *Grand Cardinal*, into Saint John harbour and bombarded Fort La Tour. Jacqueline replied effectively with her cannon and the *Grand Cardinal* was driven off with serious damage. D'Aulnay retreated to Port-Royal, repaired his vessel and returned in April. This time he landed artillery and pounded the fort from the safety of the shore for three days. On Easter Sunday 1645, d'Aulnay's men forced their way through the walls and Jacqueline La Tour surrendered, on the understanding that her

A tragic moment in Canada's early history: Charles d'Aulnay hangs La Tour's men in Saint John while Madame La Tour watches, April 13, 1645.
Painting by A.S. Scott

men would be spared. Instead, d'Aulnay hanged most of them and forced Madame La Tour to watch: she died three weeks later. Charles accepted the outcome — for the moment — and retreated to Quebec.

But d'Aulnay's victory in Saint John did not stop the fighting. He had another rival in the area, Nicholas Denys, whose commercial interests ranged around peninsular Nova Scotia, Cape Breton, and well into the Gulf of St. Lawrence. In the 1640s, Denys, too, fell afoul of d'Aulnay, who burned his rival's post on Miscou Island in northern New Brunswick. Denys returned to France and for the moment d'Aulnay was the ruler of Acadia.

When it was learned in 1650 that d'Aulnay had drowned in a canoeing accident, both Charles La Tour and Nicholas Denys came back to Acadia to reclaim their losses. Denys re-established himself at St. Pierre on Cape Breton Island, where he was arrested by d'Aulnay's widow and briefly incarcerated in Quebec City. After his release, Denys established a post at Nepisiquit (Bathurst) in northern New Brunswick in 1652. It was there, a year later, that Denys was ambushed by d'Aulnay's principal creditor, Emmanuel Le Borgne, who had arrived in Acadia to recover his investment. Le Borgne brought Denys in chains to Port-Royal. In the process of his capture, however, Denys sent a warning to Charles La Tour, who was able to prepare his fort at Saint John for imminent attack. In 1654 Le Borgne duly laid siege to Fort La Tour, but while engaged there, his prisoner Denys in Port-Royal escaped to France. There, he bought the *Compagnie de la Nouvelle-France*, with rights extending from Cape Canso to the Gaspé, and returned to Cape Breton to renew his business activities.

Charles La Tour was not so fortunate. He held off the siege, but the day after Le Borgne's forces decamped for Port-Royal, Robert Sedgewick arrived.

A New England privateer with a letter of marque from Oliver Cromwell's government in England, Sedgewick was charged with eliminating French privateers who were helping the Dutch in their war against the English. Exhausted by Le Borgne's siege, the garrison at Fort La Tour surrendered quickly to the English forces. Sedgewick subsequently took Port-Royal and most of Acadia, though not Cape Breton or Denys' establishments.

Sedgewick's conquest ended Charles La Tour's efforts to control commercial activity in what is now southern New Brunswick. He resolved his longstanding problems with d'Aulnay's estate by marrying d'Aulnay's widow, selling all his commercial interests to the new English governor of Acadia, and retiring to Cape Sable, Nova Scotia. Nicholas Denys eventually retired to his trading post at Nepisiquit, where he authored the most important written record of early Acadia and died quietly in 1688 at the great age of eighty-nine.

For the next century and more, the tides of war continued to lap at New Brunswick's shores. The French built forts along the St. John River to protect their claims and commercial interests. None of these stopped a force of over a hundred Dutch privateers under Jurriaen Aernoutsz from entering the river, burning Fort Jemseg, and cruising as far as present-day Fredericton in 1674. Nor did forts along the lower St. John River stop the Yankee privateer Benjamin Church from sailing up to Fredericton and laying siege—albeit briefly—to Fort Nashwaak in 1697.

Raids by privateers during the seventeenth and eighteenth centuries speak to the nature of the settlement by Europeans and to the commercial value of the region and its place between the larger and more commercially advanced settlements in New England and along the St. Lawrence River. For much of this period, New Brunswick was a sparsely settled but important middle ground. Most Acadians were settled in what is now Nova Scotia: farmers who were an important source of produce for New England and New France. The largest Acadian settlement, Port-Royal, was also an important base for privateering operations against the English.

During the two great wars that raged between England (Great Britain after 1704) and France from 1690 to 1713, Port-Royal became "The Dunkerque of North America"—a reference to the main base for French privateers on the English Channel. Port-Royal-based privateers preyed on both British trade to America and New England fishermen. Several of these enterprising French and Acadian sailors had New Brunswick connections.

One of them was Pierre Maisonnat dit Baptiste, a native of Bergerac, France. Maisonnat came out to Port-Royal around 1690 and participated in both King William's War (1689-1697) and the War of the Spanish Succession (1701-1713) as a privateer. After participating in attacks on the New England fishing fleet in the Bay of Fundy, in 1694 Maisonnat moved his home to what is now Fredericton, opposite Fort Nashwaak, and continued his raiding into New England until he was captured in 1697. He was freed a year later during a prisoner exchange. He fought in the defence of Port-Royal in 1707, and then sailed on privateers until the end of the War of the Spanish Succession, when he finally settled at Beaubassin.

Daniel Robinau de Neuvillette was less fortunate. Born in Quebec in 1672, he was the brother of Joseph Robinau de Villebon, governor of Acadia from 1690 to 1700, whose capital was at Fort Nashwaak. Daniel served in Acadia in King William's War, primarily engaging in both protecting French fishing vessels and attacking those from New England. He was killed in 1702, in the early stages of the War of Spanish Succession, during a Bay of Fundy battle with a brigantine from Boston.

Acadian privateers returned to the fray in the mid-eighteenth century. During the War of the Austrian Succession (1740-1748), several Acadians — by then officially British subjects — were active as privateers and Acadian patriots. Joseph Broussard, also known as Beausoleil, a resident of Beaubassin, was sufficiently active in support of France that, by 1747, Governor Shirley of Massachusetts declared him an outlaw and offered a bounty for his head. That did not deter Broussard, who, along with Mi'kmaq allies, continued to attack the British in Nova Scotia even after the war ended in 1748, including bloody raids on Halifax in 1751.

The undefined nature of Acadia was precisely what drew the British into settling the issue. In spring 1755, a large fleet carrying over twenty-five hundred soldiers arrived at the isthmus of Chignecto to capture Fort Beauséjour. Once that bastion fell, punitive raids and campaigns designed to expel Acadians from what is now New Brunswick followed. These were invariably seaborne and riverine, pushing up the Petitcodiac, Miramichi, and St. John rivers. Although the British eventually prevailed, the operations did not always go their way. An attempt to land New Englanders at what is now Hillsborough in Albert County to burn Acadian farms and expel the inhabitants ended in a bloody fiasco when the British-American troops were caught on mudflats at low tide and shot to pieces by French and Acadian forces. The British penetration of the St. John River system was marred by the loss of the armed sloop *Providence* at Reversing Falls in Saint John and the ambush of a party of New Englanders on the Oromocto River. Meanwhile, Broussard, who had helped defend Fort Beauséjour in 1755, led the resistance to the expulsion campaign throughout New Brunswick. One of his first adventures was to join with his four brothers and, using a small schooner, attack British shipping in the Bay of Fundy. After being wounded in 1758, Broussard retreated to the Miramichi to convalesce.

The British, however, were reluctant to press their luck in the New Brunswick campaign until the larger issue of Quebec was resolved. Quebec City fell in autumn 1759, but the final fate of New France was far from decided. The British expeditionary force wintered in Canada, while the rump of the French forces concentrated at Montreal. In April 1760, the British were driven back into the fortress of Quebec by their defeat at the battle of Ste-Foy, and the exhausted armies were at a standstill. Ultimate victory depended upon which fleet — French or British — would arrive first in the spring with reinforcements. The British won the race, and the French fleet would meet its fate in the sheltered waters of the Bay of Chaleur and the mouth of the Restigouche River.

By then the remnants of Acadian resistance had settled in the community of La Petite Rochelle, on the north shore of the Restigouche River opposite present-day Campbellton. Among them were the privateers Joseph Dugas, Joseph Leblanc, and Alexis Landry (who later founded Caraquet). They had established themselves at Richibucto after the fall of Louisbourg in 1758 with letters of marque from the governor at Quebec, and with several vessels began attacking British shipping around Nova Scotia. Leblanc, a farmer and trader from the Minas Basin, had a long history of opposition to the British presence in Acadia. Although a British subject, he had sailed in the War of the Austrian Succession with a letter of marque from the governor of Quebec. That ended when he was stopped by a British patrol while carrying supplies to the French at Louisbourg. He threw the commission over the side and wisely settled for a fine by the governor of Nova Scotia rather than a trial for treason. After 1755, however, Leblanc was a privateer once more, now joined by his son-in-law, Joseph Dugas. He, too, had worked both sides of the struggle in the 1740s, sometimes cooperating with British authorities, sometimes assisting the French in Cape Breton. But, like his father-in-law, Joseph Dugas was always an Acadian patriot.

Just what these enterprising Acadian privateers based in Richibucto were able to accomplish remains unclear. By 1760, the British were undoubtedly aware of the settlement at La Petite Rochelle (known to the British as the village of Restigouche), but the primary reason for the Battle of the Restigouche was to decide the fate of New France. The battle's origins lay in the departure of the French relief expedition for Quebec from Bordeaux in April 1760. The six ships carried food, ammunition, and supplies for the beleaguered garrison of New France, but only four hundred of the requested four thousand soldiers. Two of the ships were quickly captured at sea by the British blockade and a third ran aground in the Azores. Only three — the frigate *Le Machault* (500 tons, armed with twenty 20-pounders and eight 6-pounders), commanded by the very able Lieutenant de Frégate François Chenard de la Giraudais, and the merchant ships *Bienfaisant* (320 tons, with twenty-two 8-pounders) and *Marquis de Malauze* (354 tons, with sixteen or eighteen cannon of unknown size) — arrived off Bird Rock in the Gulf of St. Lawrence by mid-May. There they captured a British schooner and learned that a British fleet had entered the St. Lawrence River just days before. On May 16, the French squadron arrived at Gaspé, where they captured a further five small British vessels — all bound for Quebec with supplies for the British. The next day La Giraudais's force captured two more British ships, bringing their prizes to eight.

Model of the frigate *Le Machault*, Lieutenant La Giraudais's flagship during the Battle of the Restigouche. Model by Fred Werthman.

Lieu historique national du Canada de la Bataille-de-la-Restigouche

La Giraudais's orders allowed him to sail to the Caribbean if, upon arrival in New France, he found that the British had already arrived in the St. Lawrence River. But La Giraudais decided to find a safe anchorage at the head of the Bay of Chaleur, make contact with the governor of Canada, Vaudreuil, and await his orders. He needed to bake biscuits for his crews in any event. Besides, most of the soldiers embarked had previously served at Louisbourg and knew the area well. And so, on May 19, La Giraudais anchored his fleet in the mouth of the Restigouche River off La Petite Rochelle, landed his troops to the east at what is now called Battery Point, and established a camp.

La Giraudais probably knew that the area was a refuge for Acadians from the British expulsion campaign, but did not know that they were starving and his fleet would become a magnet for other Acadians from the surrounding area. Among those who came in was Joseph Leblanc, the most notorious of the Acadian privateers, who arrived in late June with nine prizes. Once committed to the site, La Giraudais had little choice but to stay. A runner was sent to Montreal to inform Governor Vaudreuil of the fleet's arrival, and a captured schooner was manned and sent out into the Bay of Chaleur to watch for the enemy. La Giraudais felt reasonably confident: the British had no local knowledge of the channel, and there seemed little likelihood — none, according to Vaudreuil, whose letter arrived a month later — that the British would respond with their largest ships.

But when the British learned on June 9 of the arrival of La Giraudais's ships in the Gulf of St. Lawrence, they sent an overwhelming force. Nine warships were immediately dispatched from the force in the St. Lawrence River, including *Prince of Orange* (sixty guns), *Rochester* (fifty guns), and *Eurus* (unknown), while eight more were sent from Louisbourg, including *Fame* (seventy-four guns), *Dorsetshire* (seventy), and *Achilles* (sixty), and the frigates *Scarborough* (twenty-nine) and *Repulse* (thirty-two). It was the Louisbourg squadron — seventeen hundred men and two hundred and forty-six guns — under Captain J. "Foulweather Jack" Byron, R.N., in *Fame* that ultimately fought the Battle of the Restigouche.

Fame, separated by bad weather from the rest of the squadron, was the first British ship to arrive in the bay, on June 22, and immediately captured the schooner La Giraudais had placed on patrol. Captain Byron tried to force his way into the river the next day, only to run *Fame* — a third-rate ship of the line with two full gun decks — temporarily aground. Two days later, the rest of Byron's squadron arrived. He left *Achilles* and *Dorsetshire* to guard his rear by patrolling the bay and moved the frigates *Repulse* and

Scarborough up to help *Fame* with the attack. He also armed the captured schooner, which proved to be invaluable in the actions that followed.

With the arrival of the British ships, La Giraudais prepared for battle. His force consisted of about fourteen hundred men (roughly two hundred and fifty soldiers, three hundred and seventy sailors, and the rest Acadian militia and Mi'kmaq allies) but only some fifty guns. His only hope was to fortify the river and make the British pay an unacceptable price for victory. When news of *Fame*'s arrival reached him, La Giraudais moved the merchant ships into the basin above present-day Campbellton and had a battery built and equipped with four 12-pounders and one 6-pounder landed from *Le Machault*. At that spot, now called Battery Point, the channel swings close to shore, so La Giraudais scuttled five of the British prizes to create an obstacle that could be covered by fire from the battery, which was completed by June 27. That day, *Fame*, the two frigates, and the schooner made their first attack. For the next five days, the British bombardment of the battery from the confines of the blocked channel proved ineffective. Finally, on July 3, Byron found the south channel and

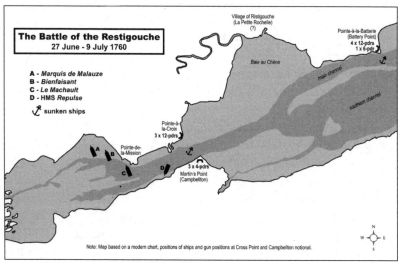

The Battle of the Restigouche. Mike Bechthold

worked *Fame* in behind the battery. Unable to reply, the battery's garrison spiked the guns and withdrew. Under covering fire from *Fame*, Byron landed two hundred men, who destroyed the battery and burned the village of La Petite Rochelle.

While the British worked to clear the main channel and lighten their ships to move farther upriver, La Giraudais built two more batteries to cover the narrows between present-day Pointe-à-la-Croix, Quebec, and Campbellton, New Brunswick. At Martin's Point (Campbellton), three 4-pounders were sited and covered by a breastwork. On the north side, at what is now called Pointe-de-la-Mission, Quebec, a battery of three 12-pounders and two 6-pounders was constructed with *Le Machault* anchored in support. Here, too, the channel was blocked by sinking captured ships. The *Bienfaisant* and the *Marquis de Malauze* (filled with British prisoners) were anchored in the channel above Pointe-de-la-Mission.

The British assault on this French bastion began on July 7. Byron put the best men from his fleet aboard the frigates *Scarborough* and *Repulse* and the schooner, which could navigate farther upriver than *Fame*. Twice, the schooner tried to force its way past the battery at Martin's Point but without luck. The issue was decided when the British towed the two frigates upriver with rowboats to bring their fire to bear on the tiny battery. By July 8, with the battery at Martin's Point silenced, both *Repulse* and *Scarborough* were within range of the French ships lying beyond Pointe-de-la-Mission.

The final act began at 5:00 a.m. on July 8, 1760, as the British frigates opened an intense exchange of fire with *Le Machault* and the Pointe-de-la-Mission battery. *Repulse*, in the lead, drew most of the French fire and was heavily damaged, with sails and masts cut down. At one point, she was struck below the waterline and sank to the bottom; as the battle ranged, *Repulse*'s crew patched the hole, pumped out the water, and refloated their ship. Most of the British fire was directed at *Le Machault*, which was similarly battered. The issue was decided when *Le Machault* ran out of powder, much of which had been landed for the shore batteries. When attempts to get more failed, La Giraudais ordered *Le Machault* and the *Bienfaisant* to be set alight.

But the *Marquis de Malauze* could not be burned. Its hold was full of British prisoners, and the French had no way to land them safely. In the event, the French simply abandoned the *Marquis de Malauze* to the prisoners — who feared that the Aboriginals would swarm aboard and kill them or that their own countrymen would open fire on the French ship. Their fate was decided by a gallant sailor who dove into the river and swam several kilometres to H.M.S. *Repulse* to report their plight. The captain of the frigate immediately dispatched nine boats to bring the men off. While *Repulse* tried to silence the battery, the boats rowed upriver, removed the prisoners from the *Marquis de Malauze*, set the ship on fire, and rowed back under relentless fire from French artillery; six men were killed in the effort.

All that remained of the French fleet now were several British prizes, Acadian schooners, and privateers, and some boats containing the supplies that La Giraudais was unable to store ashore. Byron sent his schooner and seventeen boats carrying four hundred and twenty-five men up the river to finish the job. The French burned four that were too far away to defend with musketry from the shore, but put out such a withering fire that the British were unable to destroy the remaining ten. Content that he had nonetheless destroyed the French relief expedition destined for Quebec, Captain Byron slipped downriver on July 9 and anchored.

The Battle of the Restigouche settled the fate of Canada. In the presence of unbroken British seapower, no relief was possible, and with the blockade of the Restigouche, even this remote link to France was precarious. La Giraudais managed to slip out on August 10 in a schooner carrying Vaudreuil's final dispatches. But when the Restigouche garrison tried to leave in mid-October to return to France, they were immediately met by British ships and driven back. Shortly afterward, the British passed a letter to the French commander at Restigouche ordering him to comply with the terms of the capitulation of New France, and on October 30 the garrison departed for France. Today, the battle is commemorated at the Battle of the Restigouche National Historic Site at Pointe-à-la-Croix. Two French cannon located in Riverview Park on Water Street in Campbellton recall the Gilbert battery at Martin's Point.

Many Acadians, however — especially the privateers and traders who

The *Marquis de Malauze*, used as a prison ship by the French during the Battle of the Restigouche. La Société historique Machault

survived along the Restigouche — did not accept that the capitulation of New France included them. Although the British maintained a blockade in the Bay of Chaleur, Acadians slipped in and out of the bay with ease. Typical was Antoine-Charles Denys de Saint-Simon, a soldier from Quebec, who outfitted a privateer in fall 1760 and enlisted a crew of forty-seven Acadians. A few weeks later, while capturing a small British vessel, Saint-Simon was intercepted by a British frigate and chased into a small bay near Caraquet, where he submitted. Saint-Simon went to France after 1763 and had a career in the French navy, but he left his mark on New Brunswick in the name of the village that marks the spot of his capture.

In fall 1761, the British sent an expedition under Captain Roderick Mackenzie, RN, including a frigate, into the waters off northern New Brunswick to crush this last bastion of Acadian resistance. Mackenzie's force captured many Acadian families and their vessels in Nepisiquit Bay (Bathurst) and in the small bays and coves around what is now the Acadian

Peninsula. Among those of particular interest to the British were Joseph Leblanc (and his 30-ton sloop) and Joseph Dugas (and his two brothers). Scores of Acadian vessels were destroyed and their owners and families shipped under guard to Fort Cumberland (Britain's new name for Fort Beauséjour) and Halifax to await deportation.

The British conquest of New France and Acadia ended French colonial rule in continental North America, and the lands that now make up New Brunswick became an extension of the colony of Nova Scotia. In the absence of imperial rivalries, the colony became — for a few years — a haven from the perils of the wider world. It was that stability that drew New Englanders, Yorkshiremen, Pennsylvania Dutch, Scottish, and Channel Island settlers to the region after 1763, and drew Acadians back to their ancestral lands. It also brought investment by British merchants, including one of the eighteenth century's great privateers, Commodore George Walker, who arrived at Nepisiquit in 1768.

Walker was a legend in his own day, earning a private fortune from his exploits as a privateer in the 1740s and 1750s. He was, according to author George MacBeath, "one of the most famous persons to live in today's New Brunswick." Walker began his exploits with the Dutch navy, fighting pirates in the eastern Mediterranean. By the start of the War of Jenkins' Ear in 1739, he was trading between England and South Carolina in his own ship, the *Duke William*. After helping that colony drive off Spanish pirates and privateers, and trading briefly into the Baltic, Walker took command of a privateering vessel. He was eventually captured by the French in 1745. Following his escape, Walker was given command of a cruising squadron of four large privateers: *King George, Prince Frederick, Duke,* and *Princess Amelia*. The squadron had already earned its owners some £900,000 in prize money; under Walker's command, it earned £400,000 more — a spectacular sum.

It is a reflection of Walker's drive and determination as a privateer that, on October 6, 1747, off Cape St. Vincent, Spain, while in command of *King George*, a frigate-type vessel carrying thirty-two guns, he took on the Spanish seventy-gun ship *Glorioso*, which he suspected of carrying bullion from the Caribbean. After a gun battle lasting several hours, during which

King George was beaten into a wreck, the wind freshened, enabling the *Glorioso* to sail away, with *Prince Frederick* in pursuit. The Spanish ship was finally intercepted by H.M.S. *Dartmouth* — which mysteriously blew up in the midst of the action — and captured by H.M.S. *Russell*. Only then did the British discover that the gold had already been landed at Cadiz. When Walker's battered ship limped into Lisbon, one of the squadron's owners chastised him for taking on such a large vessel. "Had the treasure been on board, as I expected," Walker replied, "your compliment would have been otherwise; or had we let her escape from us with the treasure on board, what had you then said?"

Walker made a fortune from his command of the squadron, but apparently squandered it all after the war and even spent time in debtors' prison. Much of his effort after 1749 was devoted to the revival of the British fishing industry. This did not go well, and by 1757 he was bankrupt. He appears not to have found service as a privateer during the Seven Years' War. Walker next appears in command of a fishing vessel, and by 1768 had established a base of operations for fishing and trading at Alston Point on the east side of Bathurst harbour. While Walker was in London attempting to secure his land through a grant, the whole area was granted to a Captain Allen from Nova Scotia. With a loan from London businessman Hugh Baillie, however, Walker was able to buy his establishment from Allen for £600. Walker and his business associates in London built the Nepisiquit establishment into a going concern. By 1773, he was employing twenty men in fishing, shipbuilding, farming, trading, and lumbering. And he had built a battery of guns to protect the site.

In 1777, it all came to a sudden end when American privateers from the rebellious colonies to the south plundered and burned the establishment. They then moved up the Bay of Chaleur and destroyed settlements and businesses before being brought to battle off Percé by British gunboats, which sank two of the raiders. Walker returned to England and was appointed a subordinate commander to the British admiral on the North American station. He was about to lead a squadron to sea when he suddenly died. His establishment at Nepisiquit was never rebuilt; today, it is commemorated by a plaque in a woodland park.

American privateers did not limit their plundering to the Bay of Chaleur. Saint John was much handier. As early as August 1775, Stephen Smith, a privateer from Machias, Maine, captured and burned Fort Frederick and captured the brig *Loyal Briton*, which was loaded with supplies for the Boston garrison. The following spring, despite appeals from the locals for help, American privateers were able to sail up the St. John River as far as Maugerville to raise rebellion among the New Englanders settled there. Later that year, a force from Maugerville sailed downriver and along the Bay of Fundy to lay siege to Fort Cumberland. The siege failed, but rebel sentiment in the area did not end. In May 1777, local rebel John Allen tried to establish himself at Saint John. In response, the British sent the sloop H.M.S. *Vulture* from Halifax to capture Allen's ships and disperse his force. When *Vulture* departed, Allen re-emerged, and the British sloop had to come back in June to repeat the work. *Vulture* had no sooner gone the second time than American privateer Agreen Crabtree — whom writer Robert Dallison describes as "a particularly nasty individual" — arrived in his schooner, the *Hannah and Molly*. Crabtree vandalized and looted Saint John, then sailed away. The British responded this time by fortifying Saint John and building a blockhouse at what became Fort Howe. When Crabtree returned in spring 1778, he took one look at the blockhouse and turned around, never to come back. American privateers would not return to the Bay of Fundy for thirty-four years.

Chapter Two

New Brunswick at War, 1812-1814

In June 1812, the United States of America declared war on Great Britain, and American privateers immediately began preying on British shipping in the Gulf of Maine and the Bay of Fundy. For the next four months, New Brunswick fought an undeclared war off its southern coast to defend local shipping from American depredations. Meanwhile, Britain — embroiled in a long-term conflict with Napoleonic France — hoped the Americans would just go away. Instead, American armies invaded Upper Canada, and in October Britain reluctantly declared war on the United States. Over the next three years, New Brunswickers and New Brunswick-owned vessels would participate actively in the war at sea, employing letters of marque entitling them to seize American shipping, while a flotilla of three small Royal Navy vessels plus a vessel owned and sailed by the colony operated from Saint John to both defend shipping and attack American ships.

Although New Brunswick was part of the most powerful maritime empire in the world, its coasts and ships were virtually unprotected against American attacks in the summer of 1812. The Royal Navy was stretched just trying to protect its merchant trade from attacks by the French, and it could spare only twenty-seven vessels for the whole area from Newfoundland to the Caribbean. Many of these vessels were small, old, or unseaworthy, and almost all of them were focused on protecting British shipping in and out of Bermuda. The US navy was not much better prepared for war in early 1812, but American entrepreneurs wasted no time fitting out privateers. Within days of the American declaration of war, dozens of captains and ship owners from Baltimore, New York, and Salem, Massachusetts, besieged their governments for letters of marque.

New Brunswick seafarers also knew the rules governing privateering. A formal declaration of war was usually followed by a prize act that allowed governors to issue "letters of marque and reprisal," which permitted private individuals and businesses to wage war on the King's enemies at sea. By the early nineteenth century, this was a highly regulated activity. "Prize courts" determined if captures were legal and if the enemy vessel's crew and cargo had been properly treated. In British North America, Governors John Coape Sherbrooke of Nova Scotia and George Stracey Smyth of New Brunswick were responsible for issuing letters of marque, while the Vice-Admiralty Court in Halifax monitored legal matters and acted as the local prize court. Once a prize (and its cargo) was awarded to the captor and auctioned off, the investors, officers, and crews of the capturing vessel received their agreed-upon shares reasonably quickly. If court costs, salvage fees, and the costs of arming and equipping the privateer were kept to a minimum, profits could be substantial: the New Brunswick privateer *Dart* is said to have earned her crew roughly five hundred dollars each during her first cruise, a considerable amount in an age when the average seaman earned fifteen to thirty dollars a month.

The news that the United States had declared war on the British Empire first reached Halifax on June 27, 1812, when the frigate H.M.S. *Belvidera* arrived with several dead and wounded aboard. She had been attacked three days earlier off Nantucket by the US frigates *President* and *Constitution* and three smaller vessels. That same day, a boat from St. Andrews carried the news of war to Saint John.

Although war with the Americans was not a great shock, many in the Maritime colonies hoped they could avoid the worst of it. On June 30, 1812, an Extraordinary Issue of the *Royal Gazette and New Brunswick Advertiser* reprinted the American declaration of war, but two days later, Governor Sherbrooke of Nova Scotia issued a proclamation urging residents of New Brunswick and Nova Scotia to "abstain from molesting the inhabitants living on the shores of the United States" as long as the Americans left them alone. To secure the goodwill of Americans, Admiral Herbert Sawyer, commander of British naval forces in North America, ordered his captains to treat any prisoners of war from the New England states with "great indulgence" and urged his men to avoid capturing small vessels of no value. Also, by offering economic incentives to the merchants in nearby Maine to trade with the Maritimes, he hoped they would be less likely to turn to privateering and would help to secure their continued trade with the British Empire. Sawyer convinced the Nova Scotia Executive Council to admit American goods duty free at Eastport on Moose Island, Maine. Then, British military, naval, and civilian authorities began to issue licences to American ships willing to carry flour and provisions to feed British troops fighting Napoleon in Spain and Portugal.

Since New Brunswick could barely grow enough to feed its own population of 7,000, let alone supply extra for British forces, it was critical that the existing trade between Maine and New Brunswick continue. Not only did the citizens of St. Andrews depend almost entirely on American flour, the market at Saint John relied heavily on American oats and hay. In return, New Brunswickers traded lumber and fish in New England markets. Neither side wanted a declaration of war to interfere with their longstanding, usually legal, commercial activities.

During the first two and a half months of undeclared war, some five hundred licences issued to Americans ensured a steady supply of flour and other provisions to British North America and the West Indies, to British troops in Europe, and to British fleets in American waters. As early as July 15, 1812, the commissariat in Saint John advertised for fresh beef for His Majesty's ships, and many of those who responded were Americans. At a time when money was scarce and British forces were offering hard cash, practical Yankee farmers felt that if the Royal Navy was buying beef it might as well be American. While some Americans balked at supplying enemy troops in North America, both the US Treasury Department and the US attorney general's office ruled that licensed trade with British troops in Spain was not illegal. Whether or not it was moral was up to the conscience of the supplier.

Despite these attempts to keep Americans from slipping into privateering, war descended upon New Brunswick almost immediately. Within days of the declaration of war, the American coast was bristling with privateers ranging from heavily armed ships of several hundred tons carrying more than one hundred and fifty men to open whaleboats manned by a few men armed with muskets. Small open boats were a particular threat in the Gulf of Maine and Bay of Fundy. Their crews were little more than brigands who extended their attacks to settlements ashore. The appropriately named *Weazel,* a small vessel out of Castine, Maine, terrorized inhabitants along the Fundy coast in the summer of 1812 with frequent raids and thefts of food, fishing gear, and even women's clothing.

The Royal Navy attempted to sweep these small privateers from the sea. In early August 1812, *Maidstone* and *Spartan* tried to seize the small Portland privateers *Mars* and *Morningstar* near Quoddy, Maine. The privateers fought back fiercely, killing or wounding twenty men before being forced to lower their flags. A few days later, the British ships *Indian, Plumper, Spartan,* and *Maidstone* sent two hundred and fifty men in five barges to capture the US revenue cutter *Commodore Barry* and the privateers *Madison, Olive,* and *Spruce.* In addition to the *Commodore Barry,* the Royal Navy took the US Navy brig *Nautilus,* thirteen privateers, fifteen ships, four brigs, ten schooners, and a sloop in the first months of the undeclared war.

In the meantime, the governors of Nova Scotia and New Brunswick were caught in a legal bind. Without a British declaration of war, they could not issue letters of marque, and so the early policing actions of 1812 were the work of Royal Navy vessels. Merchants and ship owners in both colonies protested that the navy would capture all the prizes before they could get to sea. The Nova Scotia governor's solution was to issue carefully worded letters of marque under his own authority, initially against France and the Batavian Republic (the Netherlands). This was expanded in August to include unspecified "other enemies of the King of England" in a letter issued to the famous schooner *Liverpool Packet,* which eventually became Canada's most successful privateer. Governor George Smyth of New Brunswick followed suit late in the summer of 1812 as New Brunswick began to fight back.

As the war progressed and attacks by American privateers and the small but surprisingly feisty US Navy started to interfere with British shipping, the Royal Navy began to apply a tourniquet to American trade by blockading the main ports along the eastern seaboard. Beginning with Chesapeake Bay in December 1812, the British gradually sealed off shipping southward from Rhode Island, closing the Potomac, James, York, and Rapahannock rivers. By March 1813, British warships had pushed to the Mississippi River, leaving the New England ports the last to be closed in November 1813. By then, the Royal Navy had succeeded in blockading some two thousand miles of coastline. This strategy struck at the heart of the American economy and went a long way toward turning American thoughts to peace.

One of Governor Smyth's first responses to the American declaration of war was to build a small fleet of bateaux and gunboats to defend the course of the St. John River. The river was part of the Grand Communications Route that linked the distant colonies in the interior with the sea, especially during the winter months when the St. Lawrence River froze over. The creation of a flotilla to defend the route was not a new idea: "garrison bateaux" — flat-bottomed boats about thirty-eight feet long, driven by a single sail or oars and steered by a large sweep — were already in use on the St. John River to transport supplies between Fredericton and the military posts farther upriver, and the army wanted more. In the opinion of Captain Gustavus Nicolls, Royal Engineers, "the principal defence to be made in New Brunswick, by an inferior Army [that is, the British] must be on the River Saint John and its Banks, and that by means of a superior Flotilla."

The creation of the St. John River Flotilla became official in late July 1812, and by early August eight bateaux and one large gunboat equipped to carry two 24-pounder cannon were nearly complete in Saint John. By the end of August, a further ten bateaux were reported ready at Fredericton, five of which carried a 6-pounder cannon, two had a 3-pounder cannon, and one was fitted to carry thirty troops; the details of the other two were not mentioned. By the end of September, at least fifteen bateaux were armed and ready for service. Also pressed into use as armed vessels were two St. John River woodboats—two-masted sailing vessels, bluff bowed and round bottomed, about forty-two feet long. They were designed to carry forty tons (twenty-eight cords) of firewood but also moved general cargo on the river. The two used by the flotilla had their holds decked over and were equipped with two 24-pounder carronades.

Although the flotilla was built primarily to command the river and support and move garrison troops, its first official function was to participate in the celebrations held at Fredericton on September 10, 1812, to observe the capture of Detroit. Indeed, because the Americans never attacked or even threatened the St. John River, the flotilla spent most of the war transporting troops and supplies. The records show, for example, that the flotilla was used to move a detachment of the 104th (New Brunswick) Regiment of Foot to Saint John in April 1813 and to carry a relief party to the Upper Posts (Presqu'Ile and Grand Falls) the next month. The last entry in the Royal Engineer papers relating to the flotilla is dated October 22, 1814, when some bateaux were being sent to Saint John for repairs.

In 1812, Governor Smyth was also forced to create his own small flotilla to protect shipping in the Bay of Fundy. The Royal Navy's initial response to depredations along the New Brunswick shoreline in the summer of 1812 was to assign a small, four-gun, 80-ton naval schooner, H.M.S. *Bream,* to Saint John. When she proved insufficient, Governor Smyth took matters into his own hands. In early September 1812, he purchased the former US revenue cutter *Commodore Barry*, captured just a few weeks earlier by the Royal Navy on the Maine coast and now lying at Saint John awaiting condemnation as a prize.

The ship that would become the armed sloop *Brunswicker* was constructed as a part of a twelve-ship expansion of the US Revenue Service between 1810 and 1812. Purchased at Sag Harbor, New York, in 1812 by the US government, the *Commodore Barry* was destined for service off the coast of Maine and was stationed at Eastport. The cost of the ship, including equipping and outfitting, came to $4,480.20, with most of the outfitting completed in Maine in June 1812. The surviving evidence suggests she was a two-masted sloop, or top-sail schooner, of approximately 80 tons and appears to have carried six guns, although she was pierced for ten. Although it is not known what type of armament the *Commodore Barry* carried, similar American revenue cutters were equipped with six 9- to 12-pounder carronades and perhaps some light swivel guns.

The US Coast Guard's "Record of Movements," which includes those of the revenue cutters, makes no mention of the *Commodore Barry*'s activities through June and July 1812. In early August, however, she was captured by the British frigates *Maidstone* and *Spartan* and brought into Saint John. The frigates' captains, Burdett and Brenton, were anxious to obtain the benefits of their work and get away, and local Saint John businessmen were only too willing to oblige. The *Commodore Barry* was sold to a group of the city's private citizens — William Pagan, Hugh Johnston, and Nehemiah Merritt — for £1,250, but since the ship had not yet been assessed by the Vice-Admiralty Court in Halifax, the sale was illegal. Moreover, Britain had not yet officially declared war against the United States, so all prizes taken under such conditions were automatically condemned to the Crown — no profit for anyone. The local purchasers must have been aware of these circumstances as they requested further indemnification. Captains Burdett and Brenton agreed to obtain the necessary papers through the Vice-Admiralty Court to allow the *Commodore Barry* to be placed on the British registry of ships. Perhaps being a bit more wary of the deal, Captain Burdett later refused to sign the agreement.

Despite having only Brenton's signature on the indemnification, the sale proceeded and the *Commodore Barry* passed into the hands of the purchasers. They then immediately sold the ship for their original purchase price of £1,250 to the colony of New Brunswick. Dubbed a "privateer-chaser," rather than a naval vessel or a privateer, the ship was rechristened *Brunswicker* and became the colony's first (and only) ocean-going warship. She would operate with a specially issued letter of marque charging her to protect the colony from His Majesty's enemies, particularly the United States, and to reinforce H.M.S. *Bream*. She was to observe all of His Majesty's instructions for commanders of naval vessels of war and privateers and to leave unmolested any unarmed American vessels licensed to trade with Britain.

While *Brunswicker* prepared for sea, Governor Smyth immediately

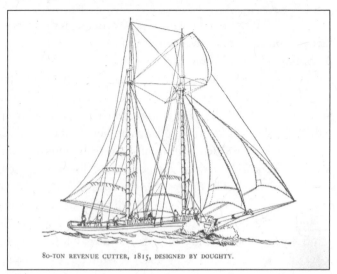

80-TON REVENUE CUTTER, 1815, DESIGNED BY DOUGHTY.

An 80-ton revenue cutter of the 1815 era similar to the *Commodore Barry*, which became the armed sloop *Brunswicker*. Drawing from Howard Irving Chapelle, *The History of American Sailing Ships*. New York: W.W. Norton, 1935

petitioned the Colonial Office in London for reimbursement of her costs, along with the necessary funds to equip and operate her. The estimates included wages for a captain, mate, and eight seamen, rations for a regular crew of ten, and sailing expenses, for a total of £1,500. In the meantime, the ship was entrusted to the care of Colonel George Leonard, quartermaster general of the New Brunswick Militia, to be fitted out with all the necessary equipment and armament to make her an effective privateer-chaser. Her first captain, James Reed, received very specific instructions on his new command from Smyth. *Brunswicker* was not to put to sea except on the specific instructions of Smyth or Colonel Leonard. While in harbour, Reed would be subject to the orders of the Saint John commandant and take actions to preserve the safety of his ship. He was authorized to recruit a first mate and six able-bodied seamen to man her in harbour and would fill that crew out to ten to put to sea. His first duty at sea would be the care and security of his vessel. He was not to engage unless he clearly had the advantage, and he was not to sail west of Passamaquoddy Bay unless engaged in an actual pursuit. In the absence of direct orders from Smyth or Leonard, he was to take such counsel as required from British naval officers in Saint John or on board ships with which he might be sailing. The expectation was that the ship and her crew would conform to the regulations of the Royal Navy, including the wearing of colours and pendants.

Money was a central concern throughout *Brunswicker*'s short tenure in the service of the colony. Captain Reed was specifically enjoined from making any purchases or incurring any debt for the vessel without approval from either Smyth or Leonard. Since there was no specific allocation in the colony's budget for the purchase and upkeep of *Brunswicker*, including wages, economy was paramount in Smyth's mind, especially given the reply, in October 1812, from the Colonial Office to his request for compensation "that so far from being able to discover in your letter any ground for incurring an expense of so unusual a nature, without the previous sanction of His Majesty's Government, I find every reason to doubt its necessity." Worse still, Smyth was specifically instructed to incur no further expense in this regard without special authorization, and if he was unhappy with the defence of the Bay of Fundy he was to take it up with the commander of the ships on station.

Faced with such requirements, Smyth became even more concerned about the expense of maintaining *Brunswicker*. While the ship lay at Dipper Harbour over Christmas 1812, the governor would allow only the paying of extra wages to a seaman for carpentry work and the cost of extra spirits for the crew when it became apparent that such an expense would not exceed that normally incurred by a British warship. Since there was no chance of her seeing service during the winter months, the request for extra seamen was denied. Smyth conceded to Captain Reed at this point that, unless *Brunswicker* was taken on by the Royal Navy, she would have to be taken out of service due to lack of funds.

The governor's concerns were quickly realized. The New Brunswick House of Assembly was advised on January 21, 1813, that *Brunswicker* would not be employed in the service of His Majesty's government. Nonetheless, and despite the rejection of his request for Colonial Office funding, Smyth submitted estimates of the cost of equipping and keeping

Brunswicker in the colony's service at its expense. The request would have added considerable strength to *Brunswicker*: ten additional seamen, a gunner (being a military man), and rations for twenty-seven men for three months. The vessel also would have had a detachment of marines.

Despite these problems with the upkeep of *Brunswicker*, she did put to sea sporadically in late 1812 in the company of H.M.S. *Bream*, and the two ships did yeoman work. In late November the pair chased American privateers off Point Lepreau and, in a separate action, drove four privateers from the Bay of Fundy; another report describes a chase under way at the same time in Passamaquoddy Bay, but this might be the same event. *Brunswicker* returned to port on November 24 and was laid up, but in December, again with *Bream*, *Brunswicker* helped establish security around the wreck of H.M.S. *Plumper*, which had been lost in a storm while carrying approximately £20,000 in coin; *Bream* and *Brunswicker* recovered £5,000. *Brunswicker* was also active in and around Passamaquoddy Bay and Saint John in March 1813. After that date, however, *Brunswicker*'s murky legal status seems finally to have caught up with her — and with Governor Smyth.

Apparently Burdett and Brenton did not take the necessary steps with the Vice-Admiralty Court in Halifax to clear up the ownership issue. In March 1813, Smyth directed the attorney general of New Brunswick to inquire into the state of the proceedings, only to discover that none had been started. Information was requested by the court in Halifax, and in May proceedings began. On June 16, 1813, the *Commodore Barry* was condemned to the Crown, in keeping with practice for prizes taken when no state of war existed. The court took formal possession of the vessel, and the short — but interesting career — of New Brunswick's first and only provincial warship came to an end. She remained tied up in Saint John until her final sale at auction on July 4, 1815.

Although the Colonial Office had not sanctioned Governor Smyth's action, there was no question that the commissioning of *Brunswicker* in summer 1812 had filled a pressing need. Newspapers in both New Brunswick and the United States eagerly noted the comings and goings of the two sides' privateers. When, in late November, the Saint John *Royal*

Gazette mentioned that *Bream* and *Brunswicker* were chasing two American privateers off Point Lepreau (by which time Britain had declared war), some twenty men from different ships in Saint John harbour offered to join the hunt. Boston's *Columbian Centinel* later told its readers that the privateers *Fame* and *Revenge* of Salem and *Industry* of Lynn had been driven out of the Bay of Fundy on November 23 by *Bream* and the sloop *"New Brunswick,"* and that their fate was unknown. In fact, the *Revenge* was captured on December 4 by H.M.S. *La Paz* and went on to become the Nova Scotia privateer *Retaliation*.

Brunswicker was not the only vessel Smyth commissioned in 1812. The fourteen-gun sloop *Comet* under Captain John Eddington was also engaged for escort duty during the undeclared war. It did not take her long to get into action. The Saint John *Royal Gazette* of September 14, 1812, published a segment of *Comet*'s log from September 10-11 describing an attack by the American privateer *Teazer* of New York. According to *Comet*'s log, she was escorting the ship *Ned*, a 400-ton, copper-bottomed cargo vessel with a crew of sixteen, bound for Saint John from Glasgow, when an unidentified ship approached flying one too many British flags. Suspicious, *Comet* and the *Ned* exchanged shots with the vessel before it finally ran up the American flag and threatened to board the *Ned*. Eddington "gave him our seven larboard guns, which made him heave about, and prevented him from boarding." After a brief chase, *Comet* watched the *Teazer* haul down her colours and "set all sail before the wind." In return for their efforts, the *Ned* sent *Comet* two barrels of gunpowder.

A few weeks later, *Comet*'s Saint John owners, Messrs. John Black and Company, advertised "generous wages" for twenty able-bodied seamen and landsmen to complete *Comet*'s crew for her next cruise under Captain Eddington. No more is heard of *Comet*, leaving one wondering whether she continued to sail as a letter of marque or was eventually captured.

We do know, however, what happened to the *Ned* after she left Saint John in fall 1812 with a cargo of lumber and no escort: she fell prey to the Salem privateer *Revenge*. At 57 tons, the *Revenge* was puny by comparison, but she carried many more men than the *Ned* and they were undaunted by the enormous size of their potential prize. The *Ned*'s crew made the best of it. After a five-hour chase that started off Grand Manan, the two vessels finally engaged in a three-hour exchange of fire that ended with the rigging and sails of both vessels cut to shreds and the privateer nearly out of ammunition. But after all that the spectre of a dozen privateersmen armed with pistols and cutlasses preparing to board her was too much for the *Ned*'s beleaguered little crew and she struck her colours. The *Revenge*, in her turn, was captured on December 4, 1812, by H.M.S. *La Paz* and sent to Halifax as a prize. Bought by Liverpool, Nova Scotia, businessmen, she went back to sea as the privateer *Retaliation*.

At the end of 1812, Smyth augmented his little fleet with a second privateer-chaser, the armed schooner *Hunter*, on loan from the superintendent of trade and fisheries. She was used to escort vessels through the gauntlet of American privateers hovering around the Bay of Fundy and the Nova Scotia coast. On Christmas Eve *Hunter* arrived in Halifax with a brig from Saint John, and on December 30, citing "Intelligence from Eastport," the *Boston Patriot* reported her back at Saint John with a convoy from Halifax. With no prizes to her credit and no further references after 1812, *Hunter* also seems either to have retired or returned to her original duties. Perhaps she, too, was caught up in the Colonial Office's failure to fund Smyth's fleet.

Although Royal Navy ships captured at least half the privateers preying in the Bay of Fundy and upper reaches of the Gulf of Maine in 1812, a handful of colonial and naval vessels could not protect the entire Atlantic coast in the early months of the war. And so Smyth added to his forces by issuing his own special letters of marque to New Brunswick's first real privateer, the aptly named *General Smyth*. The vessel—a single-masted sloop of 48 tons, boasting four guns and a crew of sixty—represented a heavy investment by more than a dozen prominent Saint John businessmen, but they would get some of it back—eventually. On her first cruise, *General Smyth* seized two prizes: the brig *Penelope*, originally out of St. John's, Newfoundland, and loaded with a valuable cargo of rum, sugar, coffee, and molasses, was captured in mid-August 1812 from the American privateer *Orlando*, and a couple of weeks later the Maine schooner *Fortune*, with a cargo of boards and rum, was taken. Since both ships were seized prior to the official British declaration of war, however, they were condemned to the Crown, so *General Smyth*'s investors earned no prize money from her first cruise.

They fared no better on the next. The first prize taken, the *Reward*, on October 10, was carrying flour, peas, potatoes, and dried fish from Salem, Massachusetts, to Lisbon, but it was for the British army commanded by General Sir Arthur Wellesley (later the Duke of Wellington) in the Iberian Peninsula. As a result, the *Reward* was tangled in the courts for six months until both the ship and her cargo were restored to their owner. It was only after Britain declared war in late October that *General Smyth*'s crew finally took a prize they were allowed to keep: the 90-ton schooner *Lydia* on her way to Baltimore with a cargo of fish and lumber; she was appraised at £889 17s 6d.

Described in the *Boston Patriot* of October 17, 1812, as one of several "non-descript annoying machines" bothering American trade, *General Smyth* does not seem to have taken any more prizes that year. But she was back to sea in 1813 and lost one of her prizes in a dramatic action that was reported in the *Boston Patriot* on August 7. The sloop *Reliance,* bound from St. George River, Maine, for Boston, had just left port in company with five coasting vessels when she was taken by a privateer described as "*General Smith.*" A prize master and very small prize crew were put on board the *Reliance*, and the sloop, three other prizes, and *General Smyth* turned north for New Brunswick. When the American privateer *Siro*, from Portland, hove into sight, *General Smyth* and her prizes headed out to sea. The *Reliance* was unable to keep up, and as she fell farther behind her original captain wrested the sword from the prize master, secured him, and brought the *Reliance* into Portland.

New Brunswickers refused to stand idle following the American declaration of war. Licences, letters of marque, and illicit trade helped keep the colonial economy going until Britain declared war in October. One vessel that was issued a letter of marque was *Union*, a small one-gun ship owned by George Younghusband, Samuel Miles, William R. Boyd, and John Atkinson of Saint John. On November 20, 1812, Atkinson and William Ward, both merchants, posted a £1,500 bond for the vessel's good behaviour. Given its diminutive size and armament, *Union* was clearly meant to be an armed trader, concentrating on normal commerce but eligible to capture prizes of opportunity, and does not appear to have captured any ships.

Another New Brunswick privateer was *Sir John Sherbrooke*, formerly the 187-ton American brigantine *Vernon*. She was purchased by brothers Robert and William Pagan and William Ritchie of Saint John and outfitted as an armed trader with a powerful armament of twelve guns and a crew of thirty. Although *Sir John Sherbrooke* was registered in New Brunswick, her bond was put up by Halifax merchants William Lawson, Enos Collins, and Joseph Allison, who had interests in a number of Nova Scotia privateers. Commissioned at the end of November 1812 under Master Thomas Robson of Saint John, the privateer seems to have made just a single trip to Jamaica via Bermuda, returning home in March 1813 without a prize. In February 1813, Collins and Allison posted a bond for a second, much more successful privateer, also named *Sir John Sherbrooke,* this one a 273-ton brigantine that had once been the American privateer *Thorn* from Marblehead, Massachusetts. After March 1813, it was this *Sir John Sherbrooke,* Nova Scotia owned and operated, that brought in the prizes.

The first—and unsuccessful—*Sir John Sherbrooke* was the last privateer to receive a letter of marque from the governor of New Brunswick. By the middle of 1813, the Court of Vice-Admiralty had seen enough dubious captures, questionable privateering, and financial practices, and had received enough letters of complaint from aggrieved merchants, to suggest that New Brunswick was either furnishing letters of marque to fraudulent privateers or her enthusiastic privateers were spoiling the traffic in smuggled goods. Whatever the reason, Governor Smyth was forbidden from issuing any more letters of marque.

Undaunted, New Brunswickers simply obtained their letters of marque from Nova Scotia for the balance of the war. The original *Sir John Sherbrooke*, for example, sailing under Captain Thomas Robson of Saint John, continued in the lucrative West Indies trade as an armed trader under a letter of marque issued by Sir John Sherbrooke himself. There is no evidence that she captured any prizes, but her distinction lies in her capture by American privateers following an intense fight against heavy odds. After departing Richibucto in October 1813, the ship vanished, and her fate remained unknown for several months until a letter from Captain Robson dated December 12, 1813, reached her owners from Kingston, Jamaica. In a matter-of-fact account, Robson explained how he had battled three ships — an American brig-of-war, a packet, and the Baltimore privateer *Saucy Jack* — "at close action for one hour and thirty minutes." *Sir John Sherbrooke*'s gunners set one American vessel on fire twice, beat the *Saucy Jack* to a complete wreck, and defeated three boarding attempts. *Sir John Sherbrooke* was on the point of escaping when Robson was shot in the head. As he reported it, "The ball entering the mouth, passing out behind the left ear, which nearly caused my death." With the mate and four others wounded and three men dead, their gallant captain now (apparently) mortally wounded, and outnumbered roughly five to one, Robson's men finally surrendered.

By early 1813, defence of British shipping in the Bay of Fundy fell largely to the armed sloop *Brunswicker* and the Royal Navy's *Bream* and *Boxer* operating out of Saint John, supported, however briefly, by *Hunter* and *Comet*. As a result, carrying the war to the enemy fell increasingly to privateers.

New Brunswick's best-known privateer, *Dart*, was commissioned in early 1813. Famous for her impressive total of eleven prizes carried into port, *Dart* is also better known than her fellow privateers thanks to the survival of a set of Articles of Agreement signed by her crew, the log detailing her two cruises under Captain John Harris of Annapolis, Nova Scotia, and her nefarious end in Long Island Sound.

A 47-ton sloop, *Dart* was small for a privateer, but her four carronades — lightweight guns of large calibre, easily handled by a small crew and devastating at short range against wooden ships — two swivel guns, and forty-five man crew made up for her lack of size. She was also aggressively handled by both her captains. By the time she was captured off Rhode Island in October 1813, *Dart* had made three cruises off New England.

Originally the American privateer *Actress* from New Haven, Connecticut,

Dart had been captured by H.M.S. *Spartan* on July 18, 1812, and had sat in Saint John harbour until April 22, 1813, when she was bought by Robert Shives, John Hay, Sr., and James Thorpe Hanford. Two weeks later they requested a letter of marque, and on May 4 *Dart* received her first commission. Her Saint John owners appointed Captain Harris, a Nova Scotian, as her first captain. *Dart*'s journal opens on May 22. Six days later, her boat chased the Eastport schooner *Sally* out of Little River only to discover that she was in ballast and had a British licence. That night *Dart* came upon the frigate H.M.S. *Rattler* escorting a prize back to Saint John. Thinking *Dart* must be an enemy privateer, *Rattler* fired two shots at her, hitting her below the water line. The frigate then realized the mistake and sent a carpenter to help plug the hole.

Dart cruised south, and the day after the epic duel off Boston between the British frigate H.M.S. *Shannon* and the U.S.S. *Chesapeake*, she seized her first prize: the schooner *Joanna* under Captain Alex Newcombe of Martha's Vineyard, apparently carrying a licensed cargo of 1,500 bushels of his own corn to Halifax. Mistaking *Dart* for the American privateer she had once been, Newcombe later claimed that he hid his British licence for fear he would be arrested for trading with the enemy. Once he was sure his captors were British, he tried to show them his licence, but Harris refused to accept it. The Vice-Admiralty Court awarded the prize to *Dart*.

Over the next few days of early June 1813, *Dart* made futile attempts to capture some small vessels, chased a suspicious sail that turned out to be an old boat not worth taking, and finally took two vessels from Portland, Maine — the *Superb,* a small boat carrying a cargo of salt, and the schooner *Washington*, "a Beautiful Pilot Boat of 65 tons burthen entirely new pierced for Guns comfortably fitted, and I expect was intended for a privateer." After manning the *Washington* with a prize crew bound for Saint John, Harris put a female passenger along with the crews of the *Joanna* and the *Washington* aboard the *Superb* and sent her on her way to Baltimore.

On June 7, after a five-hour chase and two shots, *Dart* captured the 176-ton ship *Cuba*. Prize court documents indicate that David Bishop, the *Cuba*'s owner, had obtained a licence from Governor Sherbrooke of Nova Scotia to import seven hundred and fifty barrels of flour from New York for

Halifax merchants Enos Collins and Joseph Allison and the same amount for himself and the other owners of the vessel. Because the New York customs collector was suspicious of any vessels heading to northeastern ports, Captain Bishop had used the trick of clearing for one port while heading for another lying more or less in the same direction. First, he had told the collector he was sailing for New Haven. Once there, he had cleared for Portland but, when captured by *Dart*, claimed he was actually heading north to Halifax. He complained that he had made several successful trips to New Brunswick and Nova Scotia using the same technique and had never been detained. Affidavits from the rest of the crew contradicted his statement, however, and once again the Vice-Admiralty Court awarded the prize to *Dart*.

On June 17, after nearly a month at sea, Harris decided to turn for his home, Annapolis, Nova Scotia, to get his ship in order—"the Crew Sober and some more Officers." A few days later, he changed his mind and, on June 25, *Dart* captured the *Experiment*, a small coasting sloop whose cargo of rum, ginger, sugar, tobacco, and coffee nevertheless was worth sending in. Then, on June 26, Harris spied a fast-sailing ship with eight guns per side. Nearly four times *Dart*'s size, the 230-ton *Union* was carrying a cargo of salt, fruit, and block tin from Cadiz, Spain, to Boston. It required only one shot from *Dart*'s bow gun to bring her to. Her captain readily produced a licence signed by General Wellesley in Spain, but Harris thought the tin might be subject to seizure despite the licence. Harris lost the gamble, though, and the *Union* was eventually restored to its owners. *Dart*'s first cruise ended on June 30 in Saint John harbour.

Dart's second cruise was commanded by James Ross, Harris's second-in-command. Six prizes were sent in, including the *Mequait*, out of Bath, Maine, laden with corn, rye, and fish, and the schooner *Dolphin*, heading from Portland to Boston with a load of cordwood. A third prize, the Cape Ann coasting schooner *Three Brothers,* was taken a week later. These were followed at the end of August by the Boston schooners *Hero* and *Camden,* both taken in ballast, and a schooner off Mount Desert, Maine, which was piloted through a thick fog into Machias harbour by one of its former crew. Ross's last prize to make it to court was the 49-ton schooner

Deborah, seized on September 1 while carrying corn, apples, and salt to Saco, Maine.

Dart's career as a privateer finally ended in early October 1813, after Captain Ross and his crew took a piratical turn. By the time Ross detained the ship *Governor Strong* for seven hours at the entrance to Narragansett Bay, Rhode Island, he already had a reputation as a bully. He treated the *Governor Strong*'s crew "in a most rascally manner," threatening to put them in irons and shoot the captain, and robbed the ship of five hundred dollars in cash. When *Dart* then fell afoul of the Rhode Island revenue cutter *Vigilant,* with four 12-pounder guns, two long guns firing 6-pound shot, and six swivel guns firing 2-pound shot, the Americans were content to beat the privateer into submission at long range. By the time the *Vigilant* came alongside *Dart*, the remaining twenty-two privateers and their officers begged for quarter and fled below decks without further resistance. In a final dastardly act after the Americans seized the ship, Captain Ross seized a musket and wounded a sentry. The career of New Brunswick's most successful privateering vessel was over.

But the career of New Brunswick's most successful privateering sailor was just getting started. In August 1813, following in *Dart*'s wake, Nehemiah Merritt and others from Saint John obtained a letter of marque for the schooner *Star*, captained by twenty-six year-old Caleb Seeley of Saint John, a tall, handsome sailor and every inch the gentleman. During his twenty-two day cruise in *Star* in late summer 1813, Seeley took at least three prizes, although none earned his owners enough to persuade them to continue investing. The first prize was the sloop *Elizabeth*, taken at anchor and in ballast on August 25 near Moose Island. A week later, *Star* took the 58-ton sloop *Resolution*, laden with iron ore ballast worth less than £400. The last prize was the fishing schooner *Flower*, which was bought in December by *Star*'s owner and later sold for £175.

Following his success in *Star*, Seeley invested some of his prize money as part owner and master of the Nova Scotia privateer, *Liverpool Packet*. She was already a famous vessel. Captured by the Royal Navy before the war for slave trading, the sleek, fast ship was outfitted for privateering by a group of Halifax investors. Under Captain John Barss, *Liverpool Packet* was the scourge of the New England coast in early 1813. Her capture in June by the American privateer *Thomas* of Portsmouth, New Hampshire, was a much-celebrated event. The Americans turned her around and, as the *Portsmouth Packet,* she was recaptured in the Bay of Fundy by H.M.S. *Fantome* in October 1813. Her original owners, with some of Seeley's prize money, then repurchased the ship and sent her back to sea again as *Liverpool Packet*.

Seeley proved to be a gifted privateer. His first cruise took *Liverpool Packet* off Cape Cod for a month in December 1813. In four days he captured prizes worth an estimated $100,000 and manned so many ships that he brought *Liverpool Packet* home with only five crewmen left aboard. In January 1814, he returned to the entrance to Long Island Sound in company with another Nova Scotia privateer, the ex-American privateer *Revenge*, now called *Retaliation*. By the time he was finished, Seeley sent in at least fourteen prizes in eleven months, earning the respect of both his

Saint John's Caleb Seeley, one of Canada's most successful privateers. After successfully commanding the New Brunswick privateer *Dart*, he went on to fame as captain of *Liverpool Packet*, which sailed out of Nova Scotia.
Queen's County Museum, Liverpool, N.S. (QCM)

fellow privateers and his foes. He was particularly noted for his courage, fairness in the treatment of prisoners, and gentlemanly manner. Many of the vessels he stopped at sea were allowed to proceed on their voyage simply because he had neither the men nor the inclination to take them. Under Seeley's command, *Liverpool Packet* once again became the subject of legend. In October 1814, he settled in Liverpool, Nova Scotia, and became a successful ship owner and pillar of the local community. Caleb Seeley died on Valentine's Day 1869.

Captains of other New Brunswick privateers were neither as skilled nor as lucky. The largest privateer, the 300-ton *Herald,* originally the American privateer *York Town* of New York, was outfitted as a letter of marque trader in early September 1813 with only ten guns and twenty-five crewmen. She was lost during a gale in November, driven ashore on Wolfe Island, New Brunswick, but most of her crew was saved. Captain Simmonds went on to become the speaker of the New Brunswick House of Assembly.

Hare, the ex-American privateer *Wasp* of Salem, captured two prizes in January 1814: the sloop *Hero*, laden with cordwood, and the brig *Recovery*. *Hare*'s last cruise ended dramatically and badly when she was ambushed by American sailors and some local inhabitants of Sawyer's Cove, Maine, while trying to cut out a prize from its anchorage. *Hare* got away, but several men were wounded and eventually captured. *Hare* never sailed again as a privateer.

New Brunswick's last privateer, the 160-ton Baltimore clipper *Snap-dragon,* was a famous privateer in her own right. As the *Snap-Dragon* she was North Carolina's most famous privateer, sending in prizes worth between $250,000 and $2 million — accounts vary widely. Her commander, Captain Otway Burns, is one of the state's naval heroes and his stone crypt bears one of the *Snap-Dragon*'s guns. After the ship was captured in June 1814, Messrs. Curry and Hanford of Saint John purchased her. Rechristened *Snapdragon*, she was sent off to hunt the dwindling American merchant fleet, but captured no prizes during two cruises in 1814.

It is often said that the War of 1812 was a non-event in eastern Canada, but the war at sea was significant and its history is little known. In particular, New Brunswick's connection to the naval war is often obscured by the focus on the Royal Navy and the dominance of Nova Scotia in the privateering war—and in privateering literature. But New Brunswick was fully engaged in the war at sea. Indeed, the importance of Saint John as a commercial port forced New Brunswick's Governor Smyth to raise his own fleet to defend shipping in the Bay of Fundy when the Royal Navy was too stretched to do the work. The legacy of that "independent" New Brunswick navy is the current Saint John naval reserve division, H.M.C.S. *Brunswicker*. New Brunswick's own modest, but eventful, privateering campaign was a noteworthy chapter in the War of 1812.

Chapter Three

Navies and the New Dominion

After the War of 1812, naval work along the east coast was left in the hands
of the Imperial fleet until the establishment of the Dominion of Canada
on July 1, 1867. In the intervening years, there was little in the way of
maritime conflict along New Brunswick's shore—even the Fenian scare
of 1866, New Brunswick's last colonial military campaign, was handled
at sea by the Royal Navy. But the confederation of New Brunswick, Nova
Scotia, Ontario, and Quebec a year later eventually gave the province a
new opportunity to participate in naval affairs.

The major noteworthy event in the years between 1815 and Confederation was the capture of the American steamer *Chesapeake* during
the American Civil War by a group of wayward Saint Johners. They had
been signed on as Confederate privateers in 1863 by an enterprising rebel
agent, John Clibbon Brain (an expatriate Briton), who planned to seize
the New York-to-Portland steamer and convert it into a high seas raider.
Brain and his band of New Brunswickers took control of the *Chesapeake*
off Cape Cod on December 7, 1863, and brought her north, discharging
the steamer's passengers off Saint John, where the American consul raised
the alarm. The *Chesapeake* ended up in Halifax before being handed back
to the Americans. The "privateers" appeared before courts in Nova Scotia
and New Brunswick, but escaped justice of any kind.

Confederation of the British North American colonies, indeed, was
driven in part by the fear of US revenge for their complicity in such

affairs and their general sympathy toward the rebellious South. The first international problem to confront the new Dominion was the poaching by American fishermen in Canadian waters. Since the Imperial government was not inclined to police Canadian waters at the expense of good relations with the United States, Canada briefly established a Marine Police in 1870. There is no indication of any New Brunswick connection with the force, and it was short lived—disbanded when the Washington Treaty of 1871 settled the major outstanding differences between Britain and the United States. Britain then withdrew its inland garrisons from British North America, leaving only the Imperial fortresses and naval dockyards at Halifax and Esquimalt, British Columbia.

Despite a downturn in its economy after 1867, Saint John remained Canada's most important year-round commercial port and largest urban centre on the Atlantic coast. The port city's prosperity was built on unhindered access to the sea, and it became a major regional trading centre. Its wealth derived from the resources flowing down from the vast watershed of the Saint John River, its proximity to the lucrative transatlantic trade between America and Europe, and its role as the regional trading, brokerage, shipbuilding, and commercial centre for Bay of Fundy region, stretching around the Nova Scotia coast to Lunenburg. And so it was no surprise when, during a war scare with Russia from 1878 to 1882, the Dominion government decided that Canada needed its own navy and chose Saint John as its base. On July 26, 1881, the young Dominion's first warship, H.M.S. *Charybdis*, cast her anchor in the harbour.

An aged, wooden, steam-auxiliary-powered corvette, *Charybdis* had been acquired in some haste from the British Admiralty, which had already decided that, although she was not worth repairing, the corvette would do as a training ship for a fledgling naval service. Stripped of guns and refitted, *Charybdis* left Portsmouth on June 16 and, following a rough passage, arrived at Sydney, Nova Scotia, on July 18 to take on coal. There she was met by the Canadian government steamer *Newfield*, which put aboard *Charybdis* one 6-pounder gun: her sole armament. The weary corvette's arrival in Saint John on a bleak and fog-shrouded July morning prompted one local newspaper to ask the question that was on everyone's mind, "What will we do with her?"

Historians have treated the arrival of *Charybdis* with the same bewilderment ever since, but this abortive attempt to found a Canadian navy in 1881 reflected a unique moment in history and a fleeting opportunity to start a national naval service. *Charybdis* was acquired in response to ongoing tension over Russian designs on Turkish territory. Britain and Russia nearly came to blows in 1878 at the height of the Russo-Turkish War, and the uneasiness lasted well into 1882. In Ottawa there was genuine fear that Canada's extensive maritime trade and merchant fleet was vulnerable to lightning strikes by fast, modern, steam-driven Russian merchant ships hastily converted to auxiliary cruisers.

The state of marine propulsion in the 1870s and early 1880s justified the Dominion government's concern. By the 1870s, ships were in the midst of a transition from sail to steam and many used a combination of both systems. Ocean-going, steam-driven merchant ships — especially the fast liners that carried mail, high-value cargoes, and people between North America and Europe — still carried a full suite of masts and sails for use in the event of a mechanical failure. Arming such vessels with small cannon would enable the Russians to cruise almost indefinitely under sail. Privateers had done this for centuries, but steam propulsion, which allowed a ship to attack independent of wind or tide, posed an alarming new threat. The Confederate raider *Alabama* had done just that during the recent Civil War, wreaking havoc at sea for nearly two years. No harbour, anchorage, or ship was safe from a sudden and unanticipated attack by such ships. This period of balanced sail and steam propulsion would end by the 1890s, as sail gave way completely to steam, forcing raiders to rely on coaling bases, a technological change that reduced the potential naval threat to Canada dramatically for two generations.

In 1881, however, the Dominion government was acutely aware of the danger. Moreover, the presence of scores of such vessels on Canadian registries meant that Canada could equip and train a considerable auxiliary fleet to guard its commercial affairs against potential Russian raiders,

H.M.S. *Charybdis*, the core of the Dominion of Canada's first attempt
to establish a navy in Saint John, 1881-1882. DND CN-1997

which were known to be lurking in American ports in 1880. At the time of Confederation, Canada possessed the fourth-largest merchant marine in the world. Although most of it was sail, Canada's transatlantic liner companies were also pioneers in early steam propulsion. Changes in technology began to erode that maritime power in the 1870s, but for the moment Canada remained one of the great shipbuilding and ship-owning states of the world. When the Dominion government asked Britain to take measures to protect this important trade, it was told that the Royal Navy had no ships to spare. Canada had no choice, then, but to create its own navy, and it was also no accident that *Charybdis* was despatched not to Halifax, the rock-bound home of the Imperial fleet, but to Saint John, the seat of *Canadian* maritime power.

Even the British recognized the importance of Canada's shipping fleet, both as a target and, equally important, as a source of auxiliary warships. "Looking at the very large mercantile marine possessed by the Dominion," the Admiralty advised the Colonial Office in 1878, "it is only reasonable to assume that the Canadian Government will avail themselves of their own resources for the protection of Canadian ports and shipping." In fact, the Admiralty was delighted to loan the Canadians the guns they needed to arm their vessels. By such means, Canada would quickly acquire a fleet that would "exceed in number and speed any force any European power at War with England could readily acquire on the Atlantic Seaboard." In short, for the only time in Canadian history, the size, speed, and modernity of the Canadian merchant fleet provided the basis for improvisation of a powerful and effective naval defence.

Apart from guns, what this navy-in-waiting needed most was a kernel of organization and training. The idea of a training vessel came from the commanding officer of the Canadian Militia. In 1879, he noted that there were some ninety thousand seafarers in Canada, many of whom might be trained. Some might well be enrolled in the Dominion's moribund "Marine Militia," provided for in the *Militia Act* of 1868 but never implemented. Moreover, this training could also provide a modicum of naval presence, particularly in the Gulf of St. Lawrence. In fact, under the *Colonial Naval Defence Act of 1865*, the Dominion government was empowered, subject in all respects to approval from London, to raise and man its own navy for local defence. As a result, in October 1880, the Canadian government informed London that it "would not be averse to instituting a ship for training purposes" if one could be spared. *Charybdis* was acquired to form the beginning of that naval organization.

Through the early 1880s, tension between Britain and Russia lingered over Afghanistan and India, but, as *Charybdis* rotted at her Saint John moorings, the crisis gradually cooled. The vessel's only "achievements" while in Canadian service were to damage shipping when she broke loose in a gale and careened through the harbour, and to drown two civilians, who fell through her rotted gangway while trying to go aboard.

Throughout her year and a half of idleness at Saint John, *Charybdis* became the butt of public ridicule: "Canada's White Elephant," a "rotten tub," and, to the Hon. Malcolm Cameron, M.P. for Huron, who moved in Parliament that she be sent back to the Royal Navy, a "terrible monster" that threatened only the lives and peaceful commerce of the port of Saint John. In August 1882, *Charybdis* was towed to Halifax and handed back to the Royal Navy, which scrapped her two years later. With her went all notions of a Canadian navy for a generation.

In retrospect, it is unfortunate that Canada's brief flirtation with a navy from 1880 to 1882 failed. The full impact of the shift of national economic priorities to interior development—to building railways across the continent and settling the Prairies—had yet to be felt, and, for the moment at least, Canada remained a great maritime nation. All around her, other nations were making the transition from wood and sail to iron, steel, and steam. That shift in construction was aided in other countries by naval contracts, which underwrote the capital costs of the new steel shipbuilding industries. In the late nineteenth century, Canadian investment went elsewhere, particularly into railways, and the shipbuilding industry of the east coast soon atrophied.

Throughout the balance of the nineteenth century and the early years of the twentieth, though, the requirement for local naval or policing forces never abated, especially with ongoing incursions by American fishermen. The problem forced Ottawa to establish a Fisheries Protection Service

The Honourable
(later Sir) George
Foster, January 1901:
the New Brunswicker
who played a
crucial role in the
establishment of the
Canadian navy.
LAC C004078

(F.P.S.) in 1886 and to begin operating armed vessels along the coasts and on the Great Lakes.

The father of the F.P.S. was George Foster, minister of marine and fisheries in Sir John A. Macdonald's government from 1885 to 1888. Foster was born in 1847 in Carleton County, New Brunswick, and educated at the University of New Brunswick, where he was Professor of Classics from 1873 to 1879. He was elected M.P. for Kings County in 1882 and made a minister of the Crown three years later. Foster's F.P.S. brought the Americans back to the bargaining table, as was intended, but when the US Senate refused to ratify the new fisheries agreement, the F.P.S. became permanent. In time, it would form the core of the Canadian navy, and Foster—the New Brunswick politician, classicist, and lawyer—would play an unsung role among the navy's founders.

Britain's withdrawal from its fortresses and dockyards at Esquimalt and Halifax in 1906 eventually forced Canada's hand. Naval bases and defended ports now needed torpedo boats as part of their defensive systems. At the same time, the rise of the German navy captured the attention of the Imperial government and its admirals, who consolidated the fleet closer to home. In any event, the Royal Navy was never going to protect Canada's fishing interests if it meant a diplomatic row with the United States. By the end of the first decade of the twentieth century, it was clear that Canada needed its own navy.

The idea of a Canadian navy had many origins, but it was Foster who introduced the motion in Parliament that made it happen. By then Foster, who had lost his parliamentary seat (for York County, New Brunswick) in 1900, had moved to Toronto to practise law and had returned to politics in 1904 as M.P. for North Toronto. On March 16, 1909, Foster rose in Parliament to propose that Canada formally establish its own navy. The genesis of his motion was the announcement in the British House of Commons just days earlier that the rapid expansion of the German navy put Great Britain and the Empire in peril. Germany's recent navy law committed that country to a direct challenge to British seapower in home waters. That revelation caused intense debate in the Canadian press. Some argued in favour of the establishment of a Canadian navy in order to secure Canadian interests at home, others clamoured for direct aid — perhaps the funding of battleship construction. Still others supported a third option, a militarized F.P.S.: just enough to do the policing required with no danger of foreign entanglements.

It was in this mood of public clamour for action that Foster introduced the following resolution:

> That in the opinion of this House, in view of her great and varied resources, of her geographical position and national environment, and of that spirit of self-help and self-respect which alone befits a strong and growing people, Canada should no longer delay in assuming her proper share of responsibility and financial burden incident to the suitable protection of her exposed coastline and great seaports.

In Foster's view, Canada had two options: contribute money or ships directly to the Imperial fleet, or build a Canadian naval service now. The Liberal prime minister, Sir Wilfrid Laurier, commended Foster on the spirit and intent of his resolution and recommended to the House that it "cordially approve of any necessary expenditure designed to promote the speedy organization of a Canadian naval service." Robert Borden, the leader of the Conservatives (Foster's party), further endorsed the idea, offering amendments suitable to his party, which Laurier accepted. The subsequent resolution was passed unanimously by the House before it rose that day. As historian Gilbert Tucker observed, "When the Members left the House that night, Canada had abandoned the practice which she had followed since Confederation of having no naval policy at all." Foster's Fisheries Protection Service had begun the process in 1886, and his motion in March 1909 sealed it. The spirit of cooperation and shared interest that he and his party had shown toward the Liberals' final version proved to be a remarkable moment in Canadian parliamentary history.

Unfortunately, bitter partisanship over just what kind of navy Canada would have characterized subsequent parliamentary and public debates. Most Tories wanted direct aid to the Royal Navy. Quebec nationalists wanted nothing more than a militarized F.P.S., while Laurier fought to establish a distinct Canadian naval service built around one large and six light cruisers, a naval college, and a service based at the former Imperial dockyards of Halifax and Esquimalt. The new director of the F.P.S. — and the director-designate of the new naval service — Canadian-born Rear Admiral Sir Charles Kingsmill, R.N. (Ret'd), preferred a fleet of modern torpedo boat destroyers — small, high-speed craft. Significantly, he proposed to base this fleet in three places: Halifax, Esquimalt, and an advanced station in Yarmouth, Nova Scotia. On the east coast, the destroyer fleet would guard the entrance to the Gulf of St. Lawrence during its navigation season, then shift to Yarmouth from November to May to secure the ports of Saint John and Portland, Maine, the two ports on which Canada relied the most in winter. Yarmouth quickly disappeared from the planning for the new naval service, but the importance of Bay of Fundy and Gulf of Maine ports to Canada's security remained for the next sixty years.

Laurier's *Naval Service Act* passed in early 1910 and the Canadian naval service formally came into being on May 4. Laurier proposed building a truly national naval service composed of six cruisers and as many destroyers, a naval college, and all the trappings of real navy. Two aged British cruisers, *Niobe* and *Rainbow*, were acquired for training the new service, but little else was done before Laurier lost the election in 1911, partly over his naval bill. In the years that followed, Borden's Tory government was unable to get its direct financial aid bill for the Royal Navy through the Liberal-dominated Senate; meanwhile, the fledgling Royal Canadian Navy struggled to define itself.

The one part of Laurier's navy to survive the bitter debates and strangled funding of 1911-1914 was the Royal Naval College of Canada. It opened rather informally in fall 1910 with ten cadets; the next year, it enrolled twenty-one; then, following the tumult of the 1911 election, it admitted small classes of only ten or so for the next couple of years. Among the cadets joining the class of 1912 was John Victor W. Hatheway of Fredericton.

When war broke out between the British and German empires on August 4, 1914, Canada's coasts were largely undefended. German raiders, both naval

Mess tunic belonging to Midshipman John Victor W. Hatheway of Fredericton. York-Sunbury Historical Society Museum

John Victor W. Hatheway (circled): he and three other R.C.N. midshipmen became the first combat deaths in Canadian naval history when H.M.S. *Good Hope* was sunk by a German squadron off Chile on November 1, 1914.

Canadian Naval Heritage Project, Photo Archive

cruisers and armed merchant cruisers — large merchant vessels fitted with guns and commissioned as warships — roamed the Atlantic and Pacific. The most powerful of these forces was a squadron of modern and very capable vessels operating in the Pacific under Admiral Graf von Spee. In October, the British intercepted communications ordering von Spee's squadron to attack British shipping off South America. The Royal Navy cobbled together a force under Rear Admiral Christopher "Kit" Craddock and sent it south around Cape Horn to intercept and destroy the German raiders. Craddock flew his admiral's flag from the heavy cruiser H.M.S. *Good Hope*, an aging armoured cruiser of 14,000 tons fitted with two 9.2-inch guns and sixteen 6-inch guns. Two other heavy cruisers, a light cruiser, and the armed merchant cruiser *Otranto* rounded out the squadron. Canadians became personally, and tragically, involved when, during a short stop in Halifax in August, Craddock filled a number of vacancies in his ship with midshipmen recently graduated from the Canadian Naval College: M. Cann, W.A. Palmer, A.W. Silver, and J.V.W. Hatheway. En route Craddock split his force, leaving two of the modern cruisers to guard the east coast of Southern America, and picked up a light cruiser and the antiquated battleship *Canopus*. It was a fatal error. Von Spee's modern heavy cruisers

Scharnhorst and *Gneisenau* were faster and more heavily armed (eight 8-inch guns each) than Craddock's entire force, and von Spee had three equally fast and heavily armed light cruisers in support.

On November 1, 1914, the two forces met off Coronel, Chile, in stormy seas. German fire was not only heavier, it was more accurate. The battle began at 6:50 p.m. and *Good Hope* was struck early, disabling one of her two 9.2-inch guns. In the heavy seas, the British cruisers' secondary armament—out of range in any event—could not be used because water poured in through the gun positions along the ship's side. Craddock had no option but to try to close the range. As he did, German fire became more accurate and deadly. Soon both *Good Hope* and her sister ship *Monmouth* were flaming wrecks. *Good Hope* continued to fire until 7:50 p.m., when her forward section exploded. Sometime later—there were no witnesses—what was left of her sank with all hands. Like Craddock, Fredericton's Victor Hatheway, and his three mates went down with the ship, the first combat deaths in Canadian naval history.

While the Royal Navy swept the Atlantic clear of German raiders and the Japanese navy arrived to protect the British Columbia coast, Canada sent its men overseas to fight in Flanders and Picardy. For most of the war, the naval threat in the Atlantic remained low. In 1914, the port defences of Saint John were derelict, with none of the trappings of a modern defended port, and little was done to improve them. Two field artillery pieces were quickly sent to Partridge Island, but once the German raiders were swept up the enemy threat became virtually non-existent. Only political intervention by the federal minister of marine, fisheries, and the naval service, J.D. Hazen, the senior New Brunswick member of cabinet, kept the guns on the island. Concrete mountings were built to allow them to swivel quickly to fire at moving targets.

The situation at sea changed, however, in 1917, when Germany launched an unrestricted submarine campaign against Allied shipping. Up to that point, international law and the pressure of public opinion had prevented German U-boats from sinking Allied ships indiscriminately. Submarines were too small to carry many prisoners and it was illegal to leave the crews of stricken vessels to their fate. In February 1917, however, in a desperate gamble to win the war, the U-boats were turned loose to sink Allied ships on sight. Although most of the threat was in the eastern Atlantic, a few long-range U-boats operated off the east coast of Canada. The need to organize shipping so it could be escorted through U-boat-infested waters ultimately affected Saint John. In spring 1917, the British established a system of convoys for oceanic shipping that required a Naval Control of Shipping (N.C.S.) network to manage and direct the flow of traffic. This led to the first Canadian naval establishment in New Brunswick.

On April 26, 1917, an assistant naval transport officer and a chief writer were appointed to Saint John to oversee routing of ships bound for the war zone in Europe. Since the convoy system was still embryonic and there had been as yet no submarine attacks in the western Atlantic, and since Saint John was largely a winter port, there was not much for this tiny naval establishment to do between May and November. Over those months, thirteen steamers were routed from Saint John across the Atlantic and a further eighteen to Halifax to join convoys or load coal for overseas, while thirty were routed to New York or the Caribbean. Forty sailing vessels were also handled.

Saint John's naval establishment came alive, though, on November 20, 1917, when the winter shipping season officially began. With the flood of ships shifting from St. Lawrence River ports came most of the N.C.S. staff from Sydney, Nova Scotia, including Captain F.C. Pasco, R.N., as senior naval officer, along with wireless operators from Montreal and Halifax. Several other appointments were made, bringing the total of naval personnel in Saint John at the end of 1917 to eighteen. They had a busy winter. According to their final report, shipping in the port consisted of "Naval and Military drafts, passengers, ammunition, Motor Launches for War Purposes, Material for Aeroplanes, Lumber, Provisions, Horses for Military Purposes, Chinese Coolies[1] and general cargoes." By the time the season ended in May 1918 and the St. Lawrence was reopened, 187 ocean-going vessels had been routed to Halifax, New York, Gibraltar, Sydney, Bermuda, Cape Town, and Belgium.

---

1   They had travelled across the Pacific and by rail across Canada to get to Saint John en route to Europe as labour corps.

Summer 1918 was again fairly quiet, at least as far as shipping went, until U-boats arrived in the western Atlantic, and for the first time since the War of 1812 vessels were attacked in the Bay of Fundy. The large "U-cruiser" *U-156* arrived unannounced in the Bay of Fundy at the end of July. At over 1,500 tons and armed with eighteen torpedoes and two 105mm deck guns, the sub was larger, faster, and more heavily armed than any vessels in the R.C.N. In June she had departed Kiel, Germany, with orders to mine the approaches to New York and hunt shipping in the Gulf of Maine and the approaches to Boston, Halifax, and Saint John. After laying mines off New York, which are credited with the sinking of the cruiser U.S.S. *San Diego*, *U-156* cut her way north through the American fishing fleet. The first knowledge that *U-156* was hunting in the Bay of Fundy came from some sailors who arrived in a small boat at Gannet Rock, on Grand Manan Island, at 6:30 on the morning of August 3. The men came from the Saint John schooner *Dornfontein*, and they had a story to tell.

The *Dornfontein* was a 695-ton four-masted schooner built by the Marine Construction Company of Canada Ltd. yard at Portland (Saint John) over the winter of 1917-1918. She was launched in June 1918 and formally registered in the port city on July 8. Operated by her builders, the *Dornfontein* departed Saint John on July 31, 1918, for Natal, South Africa, heavily laden with lumber. Three days later, when about seven miles south of Grand Manan, *U-156* suddenly surfaced in front of her and fired two shots across her bow. The schooner's captain was ordered to come aboard with all of his papers. He and the rest of his crew were brought on board the sub, where they shared a dinner of rice and bully beef with the Germans. Meanwhile, the *Dornfontein* was stripped of anything valuable, including food and "a large quantity of gasoline," and then the schooner was set alight.

After a five-hour stay on the sub, the *Dornfontein*'s crew was sent off in their own boats. As they rowed away, the Germans waved and cheered them on, shouting "Good Bye!" and "Good Luck!" For the *Dornfontein*'s captain, who could see the smouldering ruin of his new schooner drifting away, the sentiment was not appreciated. The Germans, he thought, "were a beastly looking set of fellows"; moreover, they had "robbed us of all we had on board worth taking." On the other hand, Canadian naval officers were none too pleased with the schooner's master. He had meekly delivered all of his papers to *U-156*, despite specific orders that they be destroyed in such circumstances. The papers included the secret routing instructions issued at Saint John for his passage to Natal. A subsequent board of enquiry suspended his master's certificate for the rest of the war. He had, it concluded, been "gravely negligent," although not with criminal intent.

In the event, the *Dornfontein* survived the incident while *U-156* failed to make it home. The schooner burned to the waterline but was salvaged. Meanwhile, *U-156* swung around Nova Scotia, sank the 4,500-ton steamer *Luz Blanca* off Halifax, then captured the steam trawler *Triumph*. The Germans put a crew aboard the *Triumph*, armed it, raised the Imperial navy ensign, then used the trawler—a familiar site along the coast—to hunt the fishing fleet further north. When the trawler ran out of coal, it was scuttled. A Canadian navy patrol finally caught up with *U-156* off St. Pierre on August 25—and promptly ran away, fearful of the enormous power of the German guns. In the end, *U-156* succumbed to an Allied minefield as she tried to pass into the North Sea on her way back to Kiel.

The presence of an enemy submarine in the Bay of Fundy was a portent of what was to come in an even greater war a generation later. The lessons for Canada were twofold: it needed a navy capable of handling such a threat, and it needed to foster popular support for the naval service itself. The officer who worked to develop these two key elements in the 1920s was Commodore Walter Hose, who took over as director of the naval service on New Year's Day 1922. Hose made two crucial decisions that affected the fate of the Canadian navy. First, he shifted ship acquisition away from big ships—like cruisers—to small, effective destroyers capable of dealing with threats such as *U-156* and its consorts. His second decision—and the first to be implemented, on January 31, 1923—was to establish the Royal Canadian Navy Volunteer Reserve (R.C.N.V.R.). The R.C.N.V.R. would give the navy a footprint in sixteen communities across Canada. Among them was Saint John.

At its founding, the R.C.N.V.R. was composed of "companies" or "half-companies." The Saint John company got under way in March 1923 when Lieutenant A.C. Wurtele, R.C.N., arrived to explain to local interest groups how the new reserve system would work. Among those gathered to hear the plan were the local Navy League, the Royal Kennebecasis Yacht Club, and the commanding officer of the local militia district. Apart from some indication of local interest, the crucial factor was space, which was offered by the local militia in the Saint John armoury at Barrack Green. A follow-up visit by the director of the R.C.N.V.R., Lieutenant H.J.F. Hibbard, R.C.N., in April determined that twenty-two-year-old Hugh Alastair Morrison, a well-known local yachtsman, would serve as the first company commander. When it became apparent that one hundred volunteers could easily be found, formal approval moved quickly. Accordingly, on June 29, 1923, Lieutenant Morrison, R.C.N.V.R., took up his command.

The Saint John company set about developing a training regime that included everything from basic drill and deportment to seamanship, navigation, small boat work, and weapons training. In the summer, the R.C.N. created a small number of opportunities for time at sea, something that might have had more appeal to R.C.N.V.R. members on the prairies than those living by the Bay of Fundy. The Saint John company failed to prosper in the armoury, though, perhaps because accommodation provided no space for social functions. In early 1924, the unit moved to Charlotte Street; then, in 1931, it found good facilities on Prince William Street. By then, it was also much smaller, and in 1927 was reduced to a half-company of fifty men after attempts by the new commanding officer, Lieutenant Paul Barbour Cross, to keep numbers up failed. The rental of a cottage on the Kennebecasis River for social activities and some training may have helped keep the half-company going during the Depression.

As war clouds gathered over Europe once again, what became the Saint John Division, R.C.N.V.R., in 1935 was the only permanent naval establishment in New Brunswick. Canada's navy then began a modest expansion, the key component of which was the acquisition of destroyers. Two had already been built in the late 1920s under Hose's initiative, and the navy now obtained five more from the British. In keeping with the practice begun with *Saguenay* and *Skeena* in 1931, all were named after rivers: *Fraser* and *St. Laurent*, which entered into Canadian service on February 17, 1937; *Ottawa* and *Restigouche*, honouring the river that forms a portion of the border between Quebec and New Brunswick (June 15, 1938); and *Assiniboine* (October 19, 1939).

The government's modest naval building program had another New Brunswick connection. In 1937, contracts were let for four steam-powered minesweepers of the Fundy class. The lead ship, H.M.C.S. *Fundy*, was commissioned in Collingwood, Ontario, on November 23, 1938. These 460-ton coal-fired vessels filled a need, but they were little more than test contracts for Canadian industry. Before the next great war was over, hundreds of ships would be completed in Canadian yards. Scores of them would carry New Brunswick names to sea, and they would be followed by their namesake communities in the greatest maritime war in history.

H.M.C.S. *Fundy*, part of a four-ship minesweeper class built by Canada in 1938 to test shipbuilding capacity in small yards and the first of a series of minesweepers that would carry place names associated with New Brunswick. Milner Collection

Chapter Four

The Second World War

The Second World War was the largest naval war Canada has ever fought. Battles raged off its coast, and the government supported the growth of an enormous navy as part of Canada's war effort. By 1945, the Royal Canadian Navy possessed more than four hundred armed vessels ranging from motor torpedo boats to heavy cruisers, with plans to acquire an aircraft carrier and squadrons of aircraft. The main focus of the navy's efforts lay in the Battle of the Atlantic: the struggle to secure the North Atlantic trade routes against enemy attack. Much of this effort was carried out by small escort vessels used to defend convoys of merchant ships from preying submarines.

New Brunswick's important, if modest, role in the war at sea from 1939 to 1945 has been neglected. Naval activity was naturally concentrated at the great naval base of Halifax and at the secondary bases developed at Sydney and St. John's, Newfoundland. No naval operational bases were established in New Brunswick during the war, although German spies and escaped prisoners of war found New Brunswick's extensive shoreline useful for their purposes.

The most important naval activity took place in Saint John, which was still one of Canada's busiest ports. Established there was the Naval Control of Shipping, which would develop to oversee shipping throughout the waters of New Brunswick, Prince Edward Island, and parts of Quebec. The port was also a crucial refit base for large vessels, including troop transports, cruisers, and battleships. The refit business kept the port's shipbuilders busy

Paul Barbour Cross, R.C.N.V.R., commander of the Saint John naval reserve unit for thirteen years prior to 1939 and one of the founding members of the naval establishment in Saint John (H.M.C.S. *Captor II*) when the Second World War started. Although old for sea service, Cross went on to command the corvette H.M.C.S. *Rosthern* in the North Atlantic and was awarded the O.B.E. in 1946.

http://www.unithistories.com/officers/RCNVR_officers.html

enough, so that little new construction took place after the first contracts were let in 1940 for a new class of patrol vessels dubbed "corvettes."

Even before war was declared, the possibility of a future Allied blockade of Europe, the threat of unrestricted submarine attacks on merchant shipping, and the importance of Saint John as a commercial port had led to the establishment of another naval presence in New Brunswick. On August 31, Captain J.E.W. Oland, D.S.C., R.C.N., Ret'd, arrived from Vancouver to assume the post of naval officer in charge of the port. He was joined within hours by Commander P.B. Cross, R.C.N.V.R., and a small staff from Halifax. Cross was no stranger to Saint John, having commanded H.M.C.S. *Brunswicker*, the newly renamed Saint John volunteer reserve unit, for the previous thirteen years. Routing, cipher work, and intelligence reporting started on September 1, while the balance of the staff arrived the following weekend. And so the basic structure for controlling movements into and out of Saint John was in place and working even as Germany launched its invasion of Poland. Saint John was also the dedicated "Contraband Control Station" for all shipping from the western hemisphere bound for Europe. Ships hoping to pass through the Allied blockade into German-controlled ports had first to stop in Saint John to have their cargoes and paperwork checked to ensure they were not destined for Germany and that they were not carrying such contraband as munitions. By the time Canada declared war on September 10, Saint John had been "at war" for nearly two weeks.

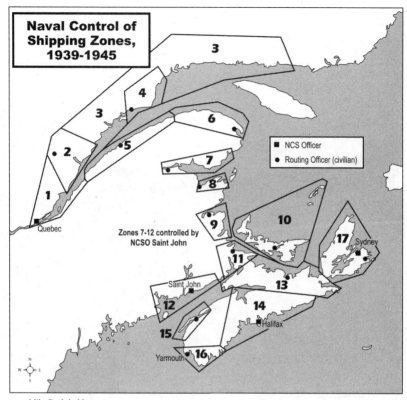

Naval Control of
Shipping Zones,
1939-1945

■ NCS Officer
● Routing Officer (civilian)

Zones 7-12 controlled by
NCSO Saint John

Quebec
Saint John
Halifax
Sydney
Yarmouth

Mike Bechthold

Captain Oland established his office at 250 Prince William Street and immediately acquired the services of three small ex-R.C.M.P. patrol boats and their crews. *Vigil II*, already in Saint John, was quickly transferred to the R.C.A.F.[1] for service as a crash boat. *Captor* and *Acadian* (renamed *Invader*) arrived from Halifax on September 5 and put in operation from Pier 5 at Lower Cove. An examination anchorage was established southwest of Partridge Island where ships could be stopped and their identities checked before proceeding into the harbour. *Captor* and *Invader* began examination services on September 19 and were supported after

---

1   R.C.A.F. aircraft, operating out of Millidgeville airport, carried out fire control for
     Saint John's coastal defence batteries.

Probably the most inelegant depot ship in Canadian naval history,
Dredge No. 2, commissioned as H.M.C.S. *Captor II* in fall 1939. DND Photo

September 25 by an examination battery of two 6-inch guns manned by the army. These guns originally came from H.M.C.S. *Niobe*, the R.C.N.'s first warship, and had been part of Saint John's defences during the Great War (both guns can still be seen in Saint John: one at H.M.C.S. *Brunswicker*, the other at the New Brunswick Museum building on Douglas Avenue). Several times during the war, a vessel that refused to stop for examination or acted strangely received a warning shot across her bow from the examination battery. Once cleared, the ships were allowed into the harbour itself.

Several other key elements of the Saint John naval establishment were added in September 1939. A site for the Port War Signal Station (P.W.S.S.) — the primary point of communication between the port and its shipping traffic and both the N.C.S. side and the harbour defences — was surveyed at Mispec Point. Until construction was completed in early 1941, however, the navy maintained P.W.S.S. staff on Partridge Island. Accommodation for ships' crews was acquired on September 26, when the old *Dredge No. 1* was taken over and commissioned as H.M.C.S. *Captor II*. In keeping with the naval custom that all establishments were commissioned "ships," *Captor II* served as the depot for the naval establishment in the port, and gave Saint John's naval base its name.

When *Captor* and *Invader* were found too small for regular and reliable duty in the examination anchorage, the ocean-going tugs *Murray Stewart* and *Ste-Anne* were acquired, arriving for duty in mid-October. That allowed *Captor* and *Invader* to concentrate on inner harbour security patrols, which they did for the balance of the war. The final layer of defences — a patrol force for the outer reaches of the harbour — was temporarily filled in January 1940 when H.M.C.S. *Cartier*, a former hydrographic survey vessel fitted with one 4-inch gun and four depth charges, arrived to patrol the bay. In the event, Saint John never had its own proper naval forces, although groups of armed patrol and escort vessels operated from the port periodically during the war.

The primary task of Captain Oland's establishment was to control shipping in and out of the port. Saint John was Canada's busiest year-around east coast port, and it possessed much more alongside-berthing and cargo-handling capacity than either Halifax or Sydney. But its work fluctuated with the seasons. While the St. Lawrence River was free of ice, much of Canada's commercial traffic moved in and out of Montreal. Between November and May, however, the bulk of that activity, including many longshoremen, moved to Saint John. Oland's first report, submitted on February 29, 1940, listed 1,187 vessels that had entered the port since September 1, 1939. Most of these were local coastal and fishing vessels, but the examination service boarded 299 foreign ships and Oland's N.C.S. staff routed 197 steamers either independently to their overseas destinations or — in the case of seventy-three ships — to Halifax for transatlantic convoys. The examination service was so busy in late 1939 that four additional vessels had to be pressed into service to handle the traffic.

Control and routing of shipping remained H.M.C.S. *Captor II's* primary wartime task. This involved close liaison with other local N.C.S. centres at Halifax and Quebec City and with the regional N.C.S. centre in Ottawa. The regional centre in Ottawa was responsible for control of shipping in North American waters — the Caribbean was controlled from Jamaica — and was linked to other regional centres and to the main British Empire and Commonwealth N.C.S. establishment in London. These centres and staffs worked closely with naval intelligence and operational authorities to find safe routes for shipping based on the latest information on enemy and Allied operations. The whole objective was to avoid the enemy, and N.C.S. staff provided merchant captains a prescribed route to follow. Knowing precisely where merchant ships were — and when they were due to arrive at their destinations — also allowed Allied operational authorities to sort out enemy raiders from regular merchant traffic and, if ships failed to arrive, to determine where enemy forces were operating. It was very much like modern air traffic control. As part of this process, N.C.S. staff issued the confidential books and special publications merchant skippers needed to travel safely under wartime conditions.

In January 1940, *Captor II* also became responsible for the use of the port by "defensively equipped merchant ships" (D.E.M.S.), commercial vessels modified with defensive equipment ranging from guns to armour plating around the bridge, barrage balloons, anti-mine equipment, and small arms. Thirty-seven D.E.M.S. inspections were done that first month and the work remained unrelenting during the war. In the early years, much of the D.E.M.S. work was focused on the large liners that called at Saint John to refit in the port's dry dock—the largest in the British Empire. Its users included not only fast troop carriers, but also smaller liners that had been converted into armed merchant cruisers. The most famous of these to call at Saint John in 1940 was H.M.S. *Jervis Bay*, which underwent a refit in July and August. She was sunk the following November by the German pocket battleship *Admiral Scheer* while valiantly defending convoy HX 84 east of Newfoundland. The Jervis Bay Branch of the Royal Canadian Legion and a monument at Ross Memorial Park commemorate her association with the city.

By the end of February 1940, Captain Oland's staff in Saint John consisted of ten officers, one hundred and nineteen men, and three civilians. They were kept busy through early 1940 as the weight of winter shipping fell heavily on the port: sixty foreign vessels routed in March, fifty-four in April. The coming of spring did not ease the work. In April, Germany invaded Denmark and Norway, and in May the Low Countries and France. Ships from all these countries scattered widely, seeking refuge, replenishment, and repair. The St. Lawrence opened in late April, but the volume of shipping using Saint John remained high. The examination battery had to stop a couple of these ships by firing blank charges.

In May 1940, the work of the Saint John N.C.S. staff was expanded to include ports along the whole New Brunswick coast and the Bay of Chaleur coast of Quebec. Much of this work was done by local customs agents and by posting naval officers to Shediac, Chatham, Bathurst, and Campbellton. Forty-one vessels were routed from these ports in July, most to Halifax and Sydney for convoys.

In May 1940, plans were also announced that the St. John Drydock and Shipbuilding Company would commence constructing a new class of naval vessels at its yards on Courtney Bay. The navy wanted fifty-four of these new patrol vessels based on a whale-catcher design acquired from Britain in 1939. At 200 feet long, displacing 950 tons, powered by familiar steam-reciprocating engines, built to mercantile standards, with a simple armament of one 4-inch Great War-vintage gun and depth charges, and fitted with minesweeping gear, these new patrol vessels would be jacks of all trades and masters of none. They were ordered to give defended ports like Saint John the rudimentary ships they needed to fulfill their function and to trade with Britain for proper warships, such as destroyers. The first three contracts for these vessels, PVs 1, 2, and 3, were let in Saint John, and work commenced on the first two in May.

The next month, Oland reported that work on PV 1 was progressing but that PV 2 was delayed by the arrival of the armed merchant cruiser H.M.S. *Laconia*, which needed urgent repairs — indeed, it was this unrelenting demand on Saint John as a major repair yard that caused subsequent contracts for new ships to be let elsewhere. As a result, these patrol vessels became the last warships ordered in New Brunswick during the war. These Flower class corvettes — as they were later known, after the name of the first of their kind — would become the iconic escort of the Battle of the Atlantic, the ships that laid the foundation of the modern Canadian navy.

By summer 1940, Saint John had settled into a routine. *Murray Stewart* and the newly arrived *Zoarces* operated the examination service, alternating four days on station and four off (in the winter they switched to three and three); both vessels remained in that service until the end of the war. *Cartier* continued her patrols of the bay, while *Captor* and *Invader* conducted harbour patrols. D.E.M.S. personnel worked on large liners and armed merchant cruisers calling at the dockyard, while the N.C.S. staff controlled the movement of vessels throughout the province and along the southern shore of the Gaspé Peninsula.

In August, the examination vessels helped calibrate new 7.5-inch guns at the Mispec Point counter-bombardment battery, and approval was received to establish a War Watch Station at Tiner's Point. Tenders for the Port War Signal Station at Mispec, planned a year earlier, were finally submitted in September, and in November, as traffic in the St. Lawrence system dwindled for the winter, activity increased in Saint John. By December, four or five ships a day were waiting off Manawagonish

The armed merchant cruiser H.M.S. *Laconia* under repair in the
Saint John dry dock. Few new ships were built in Saint John during the Second
World War due to the demand for this type of repair activity. Milner Collection

H.M.C.S. *Zoarces*, one of many ex-civilian vessels that did yeoman service throughout the Second World War as part of the Saint John fleet. DND Photo

Sackville (on the left), *Amherst* (nearly ready for sea), and *Moncton* (still on the stocks) in Saint John in 1941. They were the only corvettes built east of Quebec during the Second World War. Harold Wright

Island for berths in the harbour, which led to the establishment of a special anchorage for waiting ships.

The winter of 1940-1941 was perhaps the busiest yet. The first Saint John-built corvette, H.M.C.S. *Amherst*, was launched on December 4 with the wife of Nova Scotia's lieutenant-governor on hand to do the honours. A steady stream of armed merchant cruisers used the dry dock, as did the battleship H.M.S. *Ramilles* in late winter. Tiner's Point station opened on January 20, 1941, with a staff of six and direct telephone links to the N.C.S. office. Work on the Port War Signal Station at Mispec began in December, and the station went into service on March 10 with a regular staff of four officers and five signalmen. Meanwhile, from December 1940 to May 1941, an average of seventy ocean-going ships per month called at the port; about half were routed to Halifax or Sydney for transatlantic convoys.

Summer 1941 was quieter than normal, and even the number of ships clearing from ports in the Gulf of St. Lawrence was down. The reason for this is unclear, but by spring 1941 the war had settled into something of a routine. The intense battles with packs of U-boats in the North Atlantic over the previous winter had subsided, and in late June Germany invaded the Soviet Union, shifting almost everyone's focus eastward. Whatever the reason, the tides of war carried fewer merchant ships to Saint John and other New Brunswick ports in 1941.

The dockyard, however, was busier than ever, repairing damage caused by winter storms and enemy action. By August, there were seven vessels in dry dock and three more berthed alongside waiting their turn. The second of the corvettes, H.M.C.S. *Sackville*, was launched in May. In July, *Amherst* underwent sea trials, while a third corvette, *Moncton*, rose slowly on her slip, delayed by repair work on other vessels. Meanwhile, the local naval establishment complained about too few harbour craft and the lack of a patrol vessel in the area. *Cartier* returned to Halifax in the summer and was soon condemned and discarded. H.M.C.S. *Husky*, a former yacht, arrived in September to take up patrol work, but one small, poorly armed vessel was hardly sufficient.

N.C.S. Saint John also dealt with crew trouble on foreign vessels. In peacetime, legal jurisdiction over foreign nationals on foreign-flagged vessels was limited. During the war, it was imperative to keep ships moving efficiently, so it became necessary to implement legal means to allow Canadian authorities to board ships and remove and detain "troublemakers" and saboteurs. Until 1941, there was no real authority outside the Criminal Code to do so, but a new "Merchant Seamen's Order" passed in April allowed naval authorities to detain troublemakers for up to nine months or hold them in manning pools pending reassignment. The new order was invoked for the first time in Saint John in September and worked well. In time, a manning pool and proper consular facilities for foreign merchant seamen who routinely visited Saint John were also established, allowing for a more efficient handling of crew problems. Until then, the seamen's "pool" was usually the local jail.

In early 1942, the establishment of a Naval Boarding Service (N.B.S.) in Saint John also helped to tackle problems with crews, potential sabotage, and living and working conditions. The N.B.S. boarded vessels to check their equipment, ascertain their mechanical condition, and provide the crew personal comforts — magazines, woollen hats, mittens, soap, and so on. This general "police" work helped ensure the smooth flow of traffic through the ports under Saint John's jurisdiction. By 1942, the N.B.S.'s station wagon was logging a thousand miles or more a month visiting them.

The third winter of the war brought profound changes to the war at sea and, therefore, to the New Brunswick coast. The Japanese surprise attack on Pearl Harbor on December 7, 1941, thrust the Americans into the war and precipitated a sudden declaration of war on the United States by Nazi Germany two days later. The entire North Atlantic now became a war zone. The appearance of U-boats in the western Atlantic at the end of January 1942 and the wave of sinkings that followed created a tremendous increase in work for the Saint John routing staff, while crew troubles increased as merchant seamen grew wary — and weary — of submarine attacks. Captain Oland's appeals for more ships for examination service and harbour and sea patrol duties took on a new urgency. By February, he was asking for the establishment of a convoy system in the Bay of Fundy to protect traffic into and out of Saint John.

The immediate solution to the challenge of establishing convoys in the

Bay of Fundy was to use the steady trickle of small, Halifax-based escorts passing through Saint John for repairs to run an ad hoc system. Three convoys sailed before the end of March 1942, an unknown number in April, and nine in May. Many escorts passed through the port in 1942, and the last of the Saint John-built corvettes, H.M.C.S. *Moncton*, conducted her sea trials in May. By spring, however, Saint John still lacked the warships needed to protect traffic properly. While *Murray Stewart*, *Zoarces*, *Caribou*, and *Husky* ran the examination service and *Captor*, *Invader*, and *Vigil II* secured the inner harbour, defence further to seaward relied on the army's long-range guns at Mispec and on the regular traffic of small warships passing to and from Halifax. In May, so few escorts were available that the sailing of five vessels was delayed. In general, such delays were detrimental when every cargo and ship was urgently needed, but the delays in May 1942 probably saved several ships — and they certainly saved the Bay of Fundy from any intense enemy activity. That month, and for the only time in the war, two U-boats began to lurk off Saint John, instructed to probe the bay, report traffic, and attack targets of opportunity; one sub even had a spy to land.

H.M.C.S. *Moncton*. Milner Collection

The first to arrive was *U-213*, which left France on April 25 with orders to land a spy along the Fundy coast of New Brunswick and "where possible knock-off a steamer near Saint John before departure." *U-213* entered the bay on May 12 guided by inadequate charts and facing both fog and powerful tides, making her skipper anxious to complete his task and get out. The submarine passed along the New Brunswick shore, recording navigation light and markers, which were still functioning as in peacetime, and the sweeping of searchlights of Saint John's defences. By the early morning of May 13, *U-213* lay submerged near St. Martins, preparing to land Leutnant M.A. Langbein, also known in Canada as Alfred Haskins.

The German captain spent May 14 scouting the shoreline east of St. Martins through his periscope, trying to find a suitable landing site. Then, at 10:30 p.m., *U-213* surfaced and approached to within twelve hundred yards of Melvin's Beach, east of Salmon River. Shortly after midnight, an inflatable boat carrying Langbein, in full naval uniform so that if captured he would be considered a prisoner of war, rather than a spy — which would normally result in execution — and three crewmen pushed off through the gathering fog. What was supposed to be a short trip to the beach turned into a four-hour ordeal, as the Germans wrestled with the tide and struggled to find a suitable beach. Langbein was nonetheless landed a few miles east of St. Martins, and the inflatable boat returned to the submarine. On May 16, as the U-boat cleared the Bay of Fundy, the successful completion of the mission was radioed back to France. *U-213*'s mission was, in fact, only partially successful: although Langbein had been put ashore, *U-213* had attacked no shipping in the bay. The only contact with the U-boat was made by a Norwegian destroyer off Yarmouth, which attacked on May 15 without result. No hint of her presence appears to have reached Saint John. Her captain blamed persistent poor weather for his inability to find a target, but Michael Hadley concludes that German U-boat headquarters blamed the captain's "poor tactical record on lack of aggressiveness."

Langbein fared little better as a spy. Once ashore he immediately buried his naval uniform and radio transmitter and, in civilian clothes, wandered into St. Martins as "Alfred Haskins." He had been given

U-213, which landed a German spy near St. Martins in May 1942.
www.german-uboats.com/Uboat%20Photos/U213.jpg

outdated Canadian two-dollar bills and oversized American money as well. No one noticed, perhaps because, as Langbein later explained, he quickly learned to break the bills in places where few questions were asked. It also might account for his arrest in a Montreal brothel in early June for failing to pay his bill. "Booked [by the police] under a fictitious name, according to the conventions of the day for customers caught *in flagrante*," Hadley writes, "he paid his caution and was quickly released." This brush with the law does not appear to have alarmed Langbein. He had worked in Canada before the war and, as a patron of The Half Way speakeasy in Flin Flon, Manitoba—apparently often found in the arms of "Blonde Annie" and "Suede Anne"—he was familiar with Canada's laws governing prostitution.

From June 1942 until November 1, 1944, Langbein lived in Ottawa. When his money finally ran out he surrendered to the R.C.M.P., but they refused to believe his story. Further investigation uncovered his radio and clothes from the beach east of St. Martins. Langbein spent the rest of the war in an internment camp and was repatriated in 1945.

The other submarine off Saint John in May 1942 posed a much greater threat, but its failure to encounter any shipping had long-term implications for the security of the port and the Bay of Fundy. In late May, *U-553* penetrated the bay along the Nova Scotia coast, looking for less fog—which had hindered her reconnaissance of the province's Atlantic shoreline—and specifically in search of targets using Saint John. The Germans knew that Saint John had a large harbour with deep water alongside and a dry dock. But that was about it.

U-553 had already made a name for herself. Earlier in the month, she had sunk the steamers *Leto* and *Nicoya* in the St. Lawrence River, the first vessels lost to enemy action in Canadian waters. The event dominated the Canadian news and raised a firestorm of debate in Parliament. It also prompted propaganda broadcasts worldwide from Germany lauding the success of "U-Thurmann," which identified her captain as Korvettenleutnant Karl Thurmann. Unlike the captain of *U-213*, Thurmann was no shrinking violet.

After crossing the bay to Grand Manan, *U-553* arrived off Saint John harbour in the early hours of May 27 and immediately surfaced in full moonlight to give Thurmann a look. His war diary records his reactions: "Six miles off St John. Radio and navigation beacons as in peacetime. Barrage [barrier] at harbour entrance with a powerful search light which apparently is tested a couple of times at the outset of darkness. Lay stopped on the surface." Before diving, Thurmann signalled a report to headquarters, then spent the next four days watching the port. Canadian naval intelligence knew he was in the area but Thurmann's brazen use of his wireless off Saint John every night went undetected. Direction-finding stations had difficulty early in the war locating and intercepting transmissions from close inshore. As a result, there is no evidence that Thurmann's presence off Saint John occasioned extraordinary care in routing — or delayed the sailing of five ships that month from Saint John until escorts could be found. So *U-553* had arrived during a fortuitous lull in activity, which had long-term implications. Thurmann was inclined to blame attacks on shipping elsewhere for a general chill in movements in the Bay of Fundy, and he found little to report during his stay in the bay.

Nor did the defences of Saint John ever detect *U-553*, although they had their chances. In the dark hours of the morning of May 29, *U-553* lay on the surface and watched an exercise off the port. Aircraft flew low overhead and escorts steamed to within a thousand yards without ever seeing the U-boat. Thurmann put these efforts down as an exercise, and he was probably right, since there is no indication they were hunting for him. At this stage of the war, few Canadian small ships or aircraft had radar, and finding *U-553* in the darkness would have been a stroke of luck.

More important, Thurmann reported to headquarters that Saint John "is not used as a loading terminal for convoys." The "lively coming and going" of small escort vessels suggested to him that Saint John was a support base for escorts, used to "take the pressure off the convoy assembly ports."

U-553 went on to sink several ships off Nova Scotia and in the Gulf of Maine before heading home. She was the last U-boat to enter the Bay of Fundy. Thurmann's reports — totally wrong in his assessment of the importance of Saint John as a loading terminal — probably caused this abiding German disinterest. Certainly there were targets aplenty: over sixty ocean-going vessels per month between November 1941 and May 1942. It is clear that the Germans had no idea of the seasonal fluctuations in shipping using Saint John. Thurmann would have found ample targets in March 1942, when seventy-four ocean-going ships entered the port and most left unescorted. By May, the number was down to thirty-two, and outward shipping was travelling in convoy. The dense fog that shrouded the bay in June and delayed shipping that month did not help the German assessment.

Perhaps in response to the presence of U-boats in the bay, in August the first reinforcements for Saint John's small naval forces arrived in the form of two Fairmile motor launches, *Q022* and *Q084*. These 112-foot-long, diesel-powered vessels carried a 12-pounder gun and depth charges. They were limited to carrying out regular anti-submarine sweeps in the harbour approaches, but it was a start. In October, the Western Isles trawler H.M.C.S. *Anticosti* arrived to conduct anti-submarine patrols; she was joined by her sister ship, H.M.C.S. *Magdalen*, in November. These small escorts were part of a class of sixteen built in Canada to British contracts. Eight were retained by the R.C.N. and manned by Canadian crews for service in Canadian waters, including *Anticosti* and *Magdalen*. They represented a modest but important addition to the port's defences and — for the most part — its "naval force" for the balance of the war. The opening of a new operations room for the harbour in November 1942 facilitated coordination of their efforts with the army's coastal defences.

Two other significant developments in the latter half of 1942 also shaped Saint John's naval operations. In September, a separate convoy series designated "FH" began operating between Saint John and Halifax. These were never big—seldom more than half a dozen vessels—but they sailed frequently: an average of seven convoys a month in 1942 and 1943. During the first thirteen months of their operation—until the end of the 1943 summer season—seventy-five percent of Saint John's outbound shipping travelled in FH convoys. Organizing them was the role of the Naval Control of Shipping staff. Starting in September 1942, so, too, was control of all routing from ports in Prince Edward Island and Quebec's Magdalen Islands. This completed the N.C.S. network based in Saint John.

As 1942 drew to a close, New Brunswick also became involved in tracking U-boats. During the summer campaign, the R.C.N. had found that it lacked sufficient stations for tracking U-boats by direction finding (D.F.)—whereby their radio transmissions were used to plot their location. Clearly this had been the case with *U-553*, which had surfaced each night it lay off Saint John to send a signal home. The direction of these signals ought to have been plotted at Canada's six D.F. stations and *U-553*'s positions determined by tracing these to the intersection of the lines. Prior to the war, this had been done by the Department of Transportation as part of its marine communications system, and the department still operated the stations in use by 1942. But the navy needed more, especially on the east coast, to track U-boats.

So, in 1942, the R.C.N. started building seven D.F. stations of its own, including one at Coverdale (Riverview), New Brunswick. H.M.C. Naval Radio Station Coverdale opened in 1943 with twenty operator positions. It listened for selected frequencies, primarily U-boat radios, and passed bearings to Ottawa, where they were compiled with others and used as the basis for launching anti-submarine searches. The Coverdale station, like the others, was staffed almost entirely by members of the Women's Royal Canadian Naval Service (the WRENS), and commanded from 1943 until 1945 by Lieutenant Evelyn Cross. Their work was so good that even the US Navy intelligence branch sent frequent compliments. This "secret" installation survived the war and continued to do radio intelligence work until it closed in the early 1970s.

By 1943, the Saint John naval establishment had grown well beyond its

WREN Jaqui LaPointe operating an intercept receiver at H.M.C.S. *Coverdale* at Riverview, New Brunswick, August 1945. LAC PA-142540

tiny origins at 250 Prince William Street. The February report listed extensive new buildings in service at Reed's Point (near the intersection of modern-day Prince William and St. James streets), including workshops, D.E.M.S. offices, an asdic (sonar) building, sick bay, engineering stores, victualling depot, N.C.S. offices, naval stores, and a base superintendent's office. The War Watch Station at Tiner's Point and Port War Signal Station at Mispec tracked ships in and out, while the port's little fleet operated from Lower Cove. That fleet now included fourteen vessels: *Anticosti* and *Magdalen* provided anti-submarine patrols; *French*, *Zoarces*, *Murray Stewart*, and *Rayon d'Or* ran the examination services; and *Captor*, *Invader*, and *Vigil II*, supported by *Harbour Craft* numbers *9*, *15*, *17*, *19*, and *148*, secured the inner harbour. D.E.M.S. work continued on both freighters and large liners using the dockyard.

After a remarkably quiet period in late 1942, when shipping was drawn off by the Allied landings in North Africa, the port of Saint John became busy again in late winter 1943, and the volume continued to grow over the spring. In May, thirty-four ships were in the harbour, twenty-seven alongside handling cargo and six under repair. As the N.C.S. report observed, "A berth is seldom vacant for more than a few hours." The spring freshet pouring out of the St. John River made ship handling in the harbour difficult and occasioned delays. Ships calling at the port now included Swedish vessels engaged in relief for German-occupied Greece: seven were

Home of H.M.C.S. *Brunswicker* at Lower Cove (white building in the foreground) in the 1950s and 1960s before being relocated to Barrack Green. H.M.C.S. *Captor*, the wartime naval establishment, was located on Prince William Street across from the Harbours Board Building. Harold Wright

loading in May and were routed for the Mediterranean. Four ships from neutral Ireland were also in Saint John that month. And although activity in the Gulf of St. Lawrence had not yet commenced, the N.C.S. staff made an estimated 150 trips in February carrying messages to ships. February also witnessed the departure of the first Saint John-built merchant ship, the *Rockwood Park*, which sailed in FH 39 for Halifax, while the *Dartmouth Park* began engine trials in the harbour in April. The only bad news was the loss of *Harbour Craft 15* along with an officer and five ratings in April. Her wreckage came ashore on the Courtney Bay breakwater.

The Allies won a major victory in the Battle of the Atlantic in May 1943, inflicting a decisive defeat on German U-boat wolf packs in mid-ocean. That victory caused no change to the routine at Saint John, but the spring weather brought the U-boats back to nearby waters for more clandestine activity. Early that month, *U-262* arrived off North Point, P.E.I., in hopes of recovering escaped U-boat P.O.W.s from Canada. This was the first of two little-known P.O.W. capers in which New Brunswick played a central role.

The May escapade involved German sailors held at Camp 70, near Fredericton. They had used a simple but sophisticated code in personal letters home and received information cleverly hidden in packages, books, and letters to arrange a mass escape and recovery by submarine. In preparation, the P.O.W.s produced maps of their route to Moncton, Sackville, Cape Tormentine, Summerside, and Tidnish, plus disguises and the necessary Canadian identity documents. Although it was tracked closely by naval intelligence, *U-262* arrived safely off North Point on May 1 and waited for most of a week at the designated rendezvous. Unfortunately for the P.O.W.s at Camp 70, their elaborate and long-planned escape from central New Brunswick was scuppered by a completely uncoordinated — and failed — escape attempt a few days earlier by a

Harbour Craft 15, one of the vessels that patrolled the approaches to Saint John harbour; she went down with all hands in 1944. DND Photo .

prisoner who was not part of the U-boat group. The resulting increase in camp security undid the mass escape attempt. *U-262* got away safely.

Another attempt by U-boat P.O.W.s, in September 1943, went somewhat better. This time, a large group planned to escape via a tunnel from Camp Bowmanville in Ontario. The plan, code named Operation *Kiebitz*, called for the escape of seven U-boat captains and senior officers led by the famous U-boat ace Otto Kretschmer, captured in March 1941. Clever detective work by naval intelligence and the R.C.M.P. unearthed the detailed plans hidden in the covers of books mailed to the P.O.W.s. The information was photographed, and the rebound books were allowed to go forward as part of regular P.O.W. mail.

Rather than simply expose the escape plot, Canadian authorities planned to use it to trap the U-boat sent to rescue the escapees. Each escapee would be captured as he emerged from the tunnel and held in isolation. Then the Canadian media would be informed of a mass escape and, periodically, news of the capture of one or two P.O.W.s — progressively further east — would be released to maintain the fiction of the escape. German naval intelligence, of course, would be listening to Canadian radio and reading Canadian papers, so the ruse simply would confirm the success of the initial escape and the movement of the remaining escapees toward the rendezvous.

The P.O.W.s and *U-536* were to meet at Maisonette Point, the northern arm of Caraquet Bay in northeastern New Brunswick. The R.C.N. planned to set up two portable radar sets on Miscou Island to help track the U-boat, and trained a special boarding party armed with pistols, hand grenades, daggers, smoke grenades, and a long chain that would be dropped down the open hatches of the sub so they could not be closed quickly, thereby preventing the sub from submerging. The boarding party would be borne in a specially acquired lobster boat that would race alongside once the sub was on the surface. When the British complained that this was all rather a bit naive, the R.C.N. simply resolved to sink the U-boat.

The mass escape plan collapsed, however, when camp guards — who had not been informed of the elaborate Canadian counterplan — found the tunnel. Undeterred, Kretschmer's group threw its support behind

Kapitänleutnant Wolfgang Heyda, who had his own plan to slip out along a power line in a bosun's chair. But his captors discovered this scheme, too, and he was allowed to escape on September 24, 1943, and travel to northern New Brunswick by train as a "Mr. Fred Thomlinson," a geologist working for the R.C.N. He even had a nicely forged authorization signed by Rear Admiral L.W. Murray, commanding officer, Atlantic Coast. Heyda arrived in Bathurst and switched trains to Grand-Anse, then walked the final leg to Maisonette Point. After passing through the army cordon securing the point and its lighthouse, Heyda camped on the beach. *U-536* entered the Bay of Chaleur about the same time, and by September 28 was in place, waiting for the signal. Once contact was made, an inflatable boat was to be sent ashore to ferry him to the sub.

In the meantime, the R.C.N. had amassed a large force of nine anti-submarine ships — a destroyer, three corvettes, and five Bangor class escorts — to seal off the bay and trap the sub. Among these was H.M.C.S. *Rimouski*, a corvette with a radically new form of nighttime camouflage called "diffused lighting." This system consisted of sensors that read the ambient light, a network of lights positioned around the ship to illuminate it, and a control network. The intent — and the effect — was to make the ship, which would normally appear as a black shape against a night horizon, invisible at night. It was *Rimouski*'s job to slip into the bay and assume the guise of a small coastal ship.

The final part of the scheme consisted of a small group of Canadian naval personnel, led by Lieutenant Commander Desmond W. Piers, R.C.N., camped out in the lighthouse. Among them was Lieutenant Commander Sorenson, R.C.N.V.R., from naval intelligence and, recently, professor of German language at the University of Saskatchewan. Unwisely, perhaps, they arrested Heyda as soon as he arrived and passed him off to the R.C.M.P., who hustled him back to Bowmanville.

As *U-536* watched for lights from Maisonette Point, her captain grew increasingly uneasy about the warship patrolling the bay. If this was not bad enough, *U-536* received curious communications on frequencies not previously arranged using an unknown code word. Even worse, Piers's group at the lighthouse apparently sent light signals from the beach saying "*komm, komm.*" The complexity of the Canadian trap and the enthusiasm to sink *U-536* finally undid the plot. Once the temporary radar stations got a fix on the submarine, she was attacked with depth charges. Spooked by the overzealous Canadians, *U-536* headed for open water on the night of September 27 to the sounds of depth charges exploding in the distance.

Ironically, the only Canadian vessel to make contact with *U-536* in the Bay of Chaleur was a fishing boat, which briefly caught the sub in her trawl. *U-536*'s hydrophone operator could hear the vessel's winches working hard to pull in her remarkable catch. But *U-536* was the big one that got away, trailing the net from her hull as proof of her escape — at least for the moment. *U-536* never made it home; in an unrelated action, she was sunk by an R.C.N. hunting group in the eastern Atlantic.

After the P.O.W. escapades of 1943, naval activities in New Brunswick became routine for the balance of the war. Shipping out of New Brunswick, Prince Edward Island, the Gaspé, and the Magdalen Islands followed the usual seasonal pattern: busy in the Gulf of St. Lawrence in summer, quiet in Saint John; then, busy in the winter months in Saint John while the gulf was iced in. R.C.A.F. training squadrons at Chatham and Pennfield Ridge flew occasional patrols to seaward.

Saint John's naval reserve division, now renamed H.M.C.S. *Brunswicker*, also had a busy war. The new naval establishment provided training help for the reserve division itself and for the recruits who passed through on their way to active service. By 1945, *Brunswicker* had enlisted and processed 2,292 officers and men who went on to serve in the R.C.N.V.R. When a large new naval recruit base, H.M.C.S. *Cornwallis*, opened across the Bay of Fundy at Deep Brook, Nova Scotia, *Brunswicker* took charge of men arriving in Saint John by rail en route to the base via the Saint John-to-Digby ferry. When the WRENS were established in 1942, *Brunswicker* also took a lead in recruiting for them. One benefit the reserve division enjoyed was the opportunity to provide training aboard a great variety of warships under repair or refit at the dockyard.

Perhaps the biggest development in 1943 was construction of the Naval Armaments Depot at Renous, near Blackville. This had long been in the plans, as the naval depot at Halifax needed an inland reserve site accessible by rail. The depot was opened in 1944 and operated until 1978, by which time plans were under way to redevelop the site as a maximum security penitentiary (which opened in 1987).

In 1944 and 1945, U-boats returned to Canadian waters for their second — and last — campaign of the war. None of these U-boats penetrated the Bay of Fundy or landed spies along New Brunswick's shores; by comparison with events in 1942, this was a quiet campaign. The U-boats scored a number of signal successes, such as the sinking of the corvette *Shawinigan* in the Cabot Strait and two minesweepers in the approaches to Halifax harbour, but they did little to disrupt the movement of traffic. The major characteristic of this inshore campaign late in the war was the U-boats' reliance on their new *schnorkel* devices, which allowed them to operate fully submerged all the time. As a result, searching warships found these U-boats almost impossible to locate as they used the complex mixture of inshore waters, tides, and rocky bottoms to evade detection.

The emerging science of oceanography played an important role in learning how to locate these elusive submarines, and New Brunswick was involved from the outset. In 1944, the only oceanographic research operation on the east coast was located at the Atlantic Biological Station (A.B.S.) at St. Andrews, New Brunswick. Established in 1899 as Canada's first marine research station, it had moved into permanent quarters on the St. Croix River in 1908. In 1928, the station received a new hydrographer, Dr. Henry B. Hachey, a former professor of physics at the University of New Brunswick. Born in Bathurst in 1901, Hachey held a reserve captaincy in the North Shore (New Brunswick) Regiment and left the A.B.S. in 1940 to join the regiment upon its mobilization. After service overseas as the regimental adjutant and a company commander, Hachey returned to Canada in 1943 to work for the army on chemical warfare and operational research. It was Major Hachey, the oceanographer and physicist, who was seconded to the Royal Canadian Navy in 1944 to begin work on the mysteries of inshore anti-submarine warfare.

Hachey established himself in familiar surroundings in St. Andrews and began processing the data from bottom and bathythermograph (the measurement of temperature in relation to depth) surveys already conducted off Nova Scotia and in the Gulf of St. Lawrence by the R.C.N. It was Hachey who, in fall 1944, produced the first scientific studies on sonar sound propagation for Canadian waters; these formed the basis of R.C.N. anti-submarine warfare off Canada in the last winter of the War.

Hachey continued this work until 1946, when he was formally discharged from the army with the rank of lieutenant-colonel and awarded an M.B.E. by King George VI for his service. That year, Hachey became the chief oceanographer of Canada and continued to play a crucial role in the ongoing struggle to master sound propagation for anti-submarine purposes until his retirement in 1964. During that period, the R.C.N. became a world leader in anti-submarine warfare, a success that in no small way began in New Brunswick with a New Brunswick scientist.

Chapter Five

"New Brunswick's Navy"
at War, 1939-1945

During the Second World War the Royal Canadian Navy adopted a deliberate policy of naming its vessels after Canadian cities, towns, and villages. This was intended to develop a public following for the navy, but it also had a very practical purpose: communities could adopt "their" ship and provide comforts for the crews. The policy began when it was decided not to follow the British practice of naming corvettes after flowers, like *Petunia* and *Nasturtium*. Winston Churchill loved the idea of Nazi submariners, the "Seawolves" of the Atlantic, being smitten by something called H.M.S. *Pansy*. The Canadians had other ideas. As Chief of Canadian Naval Staff Vice-Admiral Percy Walker Nelles commented, "Flowers don't knit mittens!" So Canadian Flower-class corvettes (with a few exceptions) carried the names of Canadian communities to war.

As a result of this naming policy, and some other geographic connections, twenty-two of the approximately three hundred named warships in the R.C.N. between 1939 and 1945 had a New Brunswick connection. In the grand scheme of things it was not a lot, but it proved to be a remarkable group of ships with some unique distinctions. Ships bearing New Brunswick place names sank five German submarines during the war, about one-fifth of the R.C.N.'s total score: two were sunk by frigate H.M.C.S. *Saint John*, the second most successful submarine hunter of her class in the Canadian fleet. The old destroyer *St. Croix* was involved in what was perhaps the most tragic tale in R.C.N. history, while the minesweeper *Caraquet* led the flotilla that swept the approaches to the most infamous of D-Day beaches, "Omaha". And, as it turns out, the last remaining Flower-class corvette in the world — the class of ships that won the Battle of the Atlantic — was built in Saint John and named for a New Brunswick town. H.M.C.S. *Sackville* now rests, restored and preserved, in Halifax as Canada's National Naval Memorial — as honoured and cherished in Nova Scotia as she is neglected and unknown in her home province.

When the war broke out in 1939, two ships in the Canadian navy bore names associated with New Brunswick: *Fundy* and *Restigouche*. *Fundy* was one of a group of four small steam-powered minesweepers, all named for bays, ordered by Ottawa to test national shipbuilding capacity. Each contract was let to a different shipyard and all were in commission in 1938. *Fundy*, which gave her name to the class, was built in Collingwood, Ontario, and commissioned on September 1, 1938. Based on a 460-ton fishing trawler design and built to mercantile standards, *Fundy* and her sisters spent the war years operating in the approaches to major Canadian ports, usually Halifax, and had rather undistinguished careers. *Fundy*'s high point was probably her brief service — a single trip to Boston — as a convoy escort during the crisis of 1942 when the U-boats were causing havoc in the western Atlantic after the American entry into the war. She was disposed of shortly after the war ended.

H.M.C.S. *Restigouche*, in contrast, had a remarkable career. She was one of five fairly modern ex-British C-class destroyers acquired in the 1930s and dubbed the River class. These destroyers made up the core of the R.C.N. in 1939 and were its most powerful ships during the early years of the war. They were built to go into harm's way at high speed with guns blazing: *Restigouche* could make thirty-one knots and carried four 4.7-inch guns and eight torpedoes. She began her war operating in the approaches to Halifax harbour and later participated in the evacuation of the French ports in the catastrophic spring of 1940, when France fell to the Nazis. Most of 1941 to 1944 was spent escorting convoys across the North Atlantic and battling U-boat wolf packs.

During those years, "Ole Rusty Guts," as she was affectionately known,

H.M.C.S. *Restigouche*, "Old Rusty Guts," one of the vintage River-class destroyers Canada took into service just prior to the Second World War. She was one of only thirteen ships in the British and Canadian navies to see service in the Battle of the Atlantic throughout the war from beginning to end. Milner Collection

had her share of encounters. The most famous was the battle for convoy SC 107 in November 1942, during which *Restigouche* served as the escort group's flagship. SC 107, a slow eastbound convoy, was intercepted by the Germans while still south of Newfoundland. *Restigouche* and her small group of corvettes—including H.M.C.S. *Amherst*, built in Saint John—had to fight the convoy through a pack of submarines that vastly outnumbered them. During the early stages of the battle, *Restigouche* was particularly active in locating and driving off U-boats using her ship-borne "High Frequency Direction Finding Equipment" (HF/DF), the first fitted to a Canadian warship. The set had been acquired "unofficially" during a repair period in Northern Ireland the previous winter. Her captain, Lieutenant Commander Desmond Piers, R.C.N., knew that HF/DF picked up the U-boat contact reports as they located the convoys and was vital for convoy defence. So, while at the American base in Londonderry he "purchased" a set for *Restigouche* with a bottle of rum, which he plonked down on the base director's table accompanied by a comment that it would be great to fit *Restigouche* with HF/DF while she was under repair. He got it, and it helped keep the U-boats at bay during the early stages of the battle

H.M.C.S. St. *Croix*, one of the most storied ships in Canadian naval history.
She has the dubious distinction of being the first warship in history
destroyed by homing torpedoes. Milner Collection

for SC 107. But Piers's small band of escorts was eventually overwhelmed,
and the convoy lost fifteen ships during the battle, a significant event in
Canadian naval history.

Restigouche fared better in summer 1944 when, as part of a group of
U-boat hunters known as EG 12, she battled submarines off the French
coast and shared in the sinking of at least one. She also participated in a
nighttime battle with a German convoy off Brest in late summer 1944.
Ironically, her war effectively ended with a prolonged refit in Saint John over
the winter of 1944-1945. By the time she returned to service in spring 1945,
the war was over. *Restigouche* was one of only two of the original River-class
destroyers still in service when Germany surrendered. Worn by years of
continuous hard work, she was discarded and broken up in 1946.

The other destroyer to carry a New Brunswick name is among the
most famous in Canadian naval history, immortalized in books and
documentary films. *St. Croix* was the ex-U.S.S. *McCook*, acquired as part
of the British-US destroyers-for-bases deal of 1940. Canada took six of
the fifty First World War-vintage destroyers transferred by the Americans.
The R.C.N. followed its practice of naming destroyers after rivers, but as
a nod to their US origin, chose for these ships names of rivers common

to both countries, among them the St. Croix, which separates Maine and New Brunswick. Of the six old destroyers, only *St. Croix* and one other had sufficient range to do transatlantic convoy duty; she did yeoman service there from 1941 until her loss in 1943.

St. Croix was credited with destroying two U-boats. In July 1942, she sank *U-90* during a brief skirmish around convoy ON 113. *St. Croix* was patrolling ahead of the convoy, trying to locate U-boats as they approached, when she found *U-90* on the surface. After a brief chase the submarine dived, and *St. Croix* delivered four depth charge attacks. The final one produced wreckage, including human remains: conclusive evidence of *U-90*'s destruction.

In March 1943, she joined up with another "New Brunswick" ship, the corvette H.M.C.S. *Shediac*, to sink *U-87*. The two vessels were part of a group escorting a convoy from Britain to the Mediterranean. Off Portugal, while the convoy was under attack by long-range German aircraft, *Shediac* got an underwater contact. The corvette attacked with depth charges, *St. Croix* steaming to her support. Once the destroyer arrived, the two ships orchestrated a series of depth charge attacks, one guiding the other over the target while it was held in the sonar beam. Evidence of the destruction of *U-87* was slim at the time, and the ships were forced to return to the convoy. It was sometime later that the destruction of *U-87* by these two ships with New Brunswick names was confirmed.

The Germans got their revenge, however, later in 1943 when *St. Croix* earned the costly distinction of becoming the first warship sunk by an acoustic homing torpedo. In September 1943, she was part of a special submarine hunting group that included H.M.C.S. *Sackville*, sent out to help protect the combined convoys ONS 18/ON 202 west of Ireland. The U-boats attacking the convoy were equipped with new acoustic homing torpedoes, and on September 20 one of these blew the stern off the British frigate *Lagan*, which had to be towed into port. When *St. Croix* swept around the convoy later that day, one of the new torpedoes exploded directly under her keel, crippling the old destroyer and stopping her dead. The British frigate *Itchen* arrived just in time to see *St. Croix* shattered by a second torpedo. A third homing torpedo fired by the U-boat exploded in

Itchen's wake, chasing her away and leaving *St. Croix*'s survivors in leaking boats and rafts overnight. When *Itchen* returned early the next day, about one hundred of *St. Croix*'s one hundred and forty-seven officers and men were rescued. *Itchen* already had on board two survivors from the little British corvette *Polyanthus*, which had been completely destroyed by a homing torpedo shortly after *St. Croix* was sunk.

On the night of September 21, *Itchen* was in the thick of the battle and was herself destroyed in a towering explosion caused by a homing torpedo detonating under her magazine. Only three men survived that blast and a perilous stay in the water: two from *Itchen* and one from *St. Croix*. Even they would have been lost but for the heroism of the Polish steamer *Waleha*, which stopped to pick them up. Among those lost was Surgeon Lieutenant W.L.M. King, R.C.N.V.R., the Canadian prime minister's nephew.

While destroyers were the dashing elements of the fleet, most of the wartime R.C.N. was composed of corvettes — small, hastily built auxiliary vessels used for the dreary work of close escort of convoys. The first three of the most famous class of these vessels, the Flower-class corvettes, were built in Saint John and all named for New Brunswick-Nova Scotia border communities: *Amherst, Sackville,* and *Moncton*.

H.M.C.S. *Amherst* had an exciting career on the mid-Atlantic convoy routes. She began her war in St. John's, Newfoundland, in October 1941, escorting convoys across the embattled mid-ocean. In November 1942, she served alongside *Restigouche* in the escort group that strove mightily to protect SC 107. After a long refit in Charlottetown in 1943, *Amherst* returned to the North Atlantic late that year. She was assigned to the local Halifax force following another lengthy refit in 1944 but ended her war with group C7 on a round trip to the UK. Sold to the Venezuelan navy in 1946, she served as the *Federación* until discarded in 1956.

H.M.C.S. *Moncton* has gone down in history for taking the longest of any corvette — British or Canadian — to build: two years from the laying of the keel to commissioning in May 1942. She had a fairly quiet war, operating in the western Atlantic escorting convoys between New York and the Grand Banks, off Newfoundland. In January 1944, *Moncton* was transferred to the Pacific for the balance of the war. Still in good shape,

H.M.C.S. *Shediac*, built in Vancouver, and the only corvette named for a New Brunswick town to be credited with sinking a U-boat. Milner Collection

she was sold to a Dutch company for conversion to a whale catcher, and steamed on as the *Willem Vinke* until broken up in 1966.

The third of Saint John's three corvettes, H.M.C.S. *Sackville*, which took nearly as long as *Moncton* to complete, is remembered for her wartime exploits in the mid-Atlantic battling U-boat wolf packs.[1] Within weeks of becoming operational, *Sackville* was in the midst of great convoy battles. In one, around ON 115 in July 1942, she engaged three U-boats in furious battle in a single night, ramming one and damaging another. At the time it was thought she had sunk two, but both reached port. In late summer 1943, she was part of the anti-submarine hunting group EG 9, which included *St. Croix*. In the battle in which *St. Croix* was destroyed, *Sackville* narrowly missed the same fate when at least one acoustic homing torpedo detonated in her wake. Her survival was pure luck.

In the winter of 1943-1944, *Sackville* went to Galveston, Texas, for a major refit. She returned to North Atlantic service only to blow one of her two boilers shortly after arriving in Ireland on her first post-refit crossing. The navy decided it was not worth fixing the boiler, but as a

1   These have been recorded in a number of books, including Alan Easton's classic memoir *50 North*.

fully modernized and recently refitted corvette, and otherwise in good trim, *Sackville* was assigned to training duty. Then the R.C.N. decided it had a better idea for the venerable corvette: remove *Sackville*'s damaged boiler and convert her to a maintenance vessel for harbour defence "loops"—underwater cables that detected magnetic changes as ships passed over them. The space previously occupied by the boiler provided an excellent storage area for the massive cables. In this useful guise, she survived into the postwar navy.

In the 1950s, *Sackville* was converted to an oceanographic research vessel, which kept her in service until 1982. She was then transferred to a trust dedicated to her restoration and preservation. Over the next few years, her post-war superstructure, including a massive modern enclosed bridge and laboratories built on the stern, was cut away and she was restored to her post-Galveston 1944 appearance. Weapons and

H.M.C.S. *Sackville*, a veteran of many North Atlantic convoy battles, was briefly credited with sinking two U-boats in a single night; in fact, both were damaged but made port. The last of all the wartime corvettes, the restored *Sackville* is preserved in Halifax as Canada's National Naval Memorial. Canadian Naval Heritage Project, Photo Archive

H.M.C.S. *Bouctouche* in dry dock at Lauzon, Quebec, where she was built. Few photographs show better the small size of a corvette. Milner Collection

equipment were bought, borrowed, and scrounged from far and wide. By 1985—the seventy-fifth anniversary of the founding of the R.C.N.—she was ready. On May 4, in a ceremony alongside the Halifax dockyard, the last corvette, built in Saint John and named for a New Brunswick town, was officially declared Canada's National Naval Memorial and once more commissioned as H.M.C.S. *Sackville*.

Seven other corvettes bore the names of New Brunswick towns. *Bouctouche* and *Shediac*, commissioned from Quebec yards in June and July 1941, respectively, both had busy and interesting careers. In 1942, after a short stint in the broad Atlantic, *Bouctouche* was transferred to local Canadian forces and spent much of the rest of her war—appropriately enough and as seasons permitted—in the Gulf of St. Lawrence. She was discarded soon after the war and broken up. *Shediac* battled wolf packs in the mid-Atlantic during 1942-1943, before being transferred in early 1943 to the eastern Atlantic and the Gibraltar route, where she shared in the sinking of *U-87*. She ended her war in the Pacific and, like *Moncton*, was sold and converted into a Dutch whaler, the *Jooske Vinke*, as which she operated until 1966.

H.M.C.S. *Edmundston*, commissioned in October 1941 in Victoria,

H.M.C.S. *Fredericton*, one of the earliest of the second generation
of corvettes, with improved sheer and flare forward, extended foc'sle,
and better bridge. Known as "the lucky ship," *Fredericton* served in the
North Atlantic from 1942 until 1945 but never saw the enemy or fired
a shot in anger. Canadian Naval Heritage Project, Photo Archive

British Columbia, served on the west coast for a year. The high point
of that experience was rescuing thirty-one crewmen from the S.S. *Fort
Camosun*, torpedoed by a Japanese submarine off Vancouver Island on
June 20, 1942. Transferred to the Atlantic, *Edmundston* was among the
first Canadian corvettes to be modernized. That landed her a slot in the
hunter-killer group EG 5 in fall 1943, and she was engaged off Spain in
one of the first battles at sea involving German glider bombs, the world's
first guided missiles. Several ships were hit, including the destroyer
H.M.C.S. *Athabaskan*, while *Edmundston* narrowly escaped several attacks.
Replaced by even more modern vessels in the sub-hunting role in 1944,
Edmundston ended the war on close escort duty in the North Atlantic.
She was converted after the war into a small commercial steamer and
disappeared from Lloyd's Register in 1962.

H.M.C.S. *Fredericton,* commissioned in December 1941 at Sorel, Quebec,
was among the first of a new class of corvettes with revised hull lines and
improved endurance. Her initial service was escorting oil convoys from
Halifax to the Caribbean and then on the New York to Cuba route during
the carnage of east coast shipping inflicted by U-boats entirely without loss

in spring and summer 1942. *Fredericton* finished her war as close escort for North Atlantic convoys and was broken up in 1946.

Late in the war, a seventh corvette was named in honour of New Brunswick, H.M.C.S. *Atholl*. She was actually named for Campbellton, but since there was already an H.M.S. *Campbellton* on the British Commonwealth list, she took the name of one of the town's founding communities. By the time *Atholl* was commissioned in October 1943, the wolf packs had been beaten and her career as an Atlantic convoy escort was uneventful. She lay in fleet reserve until scrapped in 1952.

In addition to building corvettes, the R.C.N. launched several programs of minesweeper construction, starting in 1940. Most were of the Bangor class: 180 feet long and 672 tons. Of the fifty-four built, four carried names associated with New Brunswick. *Chignecto* and *Miramichi*, the first two, were launched in Vancouver in late 1941 as part of the second group and, rare among R.C.N. vessels, served their entire wartime careers on the west coast—years of patrolling and no action. Both were sold in 1946 to a San Francisco company for conversion to civilian use and disappeared from the record.

When the Bangor-class minesweeper H.M.C.S. *Caraquet* slid down the ways in Vancouver in April 1942, the navy was still naming these types of vessels after bays. For the fifth Bangor program, however, the navy adopted town names, and so the last New Brunswick-named minesweeper, launched in September 1942 at Port Arthur, Ontario, was named *Milltown*.

Caraquet and *Milltown* had more active careers than *Chignecto* and *Miramichi*. Both were immediately assigned to convoy escort duty in 1942 in the Atlantic, where attacks were heavy and losses high. Then, in early 1944, after refits, both joined the 31st (Canadian) Minesweeping Flotilla as part of the invasion force headed for France for D-Day. *Caraquet* had the distinction of serving as the flagship of the 31st (Canadian) Flotilla, the unit that cleared the approaches to the American beach called "Omaha"—the bloodiest of the D-Day landings. In the early hours of June 6, 1944, *Caraquet*, *Milltown*, and their Canadian sisters swept to within 1,500 metres off the bluffs overlooking Omaha beach, clearing the lanes for the assault troops of the US 1st and 29th Divisions. Once the lanes had been cleared for the infantry assault, *Caraquet* led the Canadian flotilla in clearing zones for the supporting bombardment ships and assault ships landing the reserve waves of the attack. The operations of the 31st (Canadian) Minesweeping Flotilla are now commemorated by a plaque mounted on a German gun emplacement overlooking Omaha beach. *Milltown* stayed in the fleet reserve for a decade after the war, then was discarded; *Caraquet* was sold to the Portuguese navy and served as a research vessel until 1975.

The other small ship with a New Brunswick name to enter service in 1942 was the Western Island-class trawler *Miscou*. Originally built in Montreal for the British, she was loaned to the R.C.N. during the war and spent her time with local defence forces at Saint John and Sydney. She was handed back to the British in 1945 and sold to Norwegian interests, who discarded her in 1965.

The wave of small ships ordered early in the war was soon supplemented by larger vessels, the most numerous of which were frigates of various types. In the R.C.N., the largest group of frigates was the British-designed River class, which the R.C.N. chose to name instead after communities. Of the seventy-seven frigates in service in the wartime R.C.N., five bore New Brunswick names.

The first to enter service, and arguably the most successful, was H.M.C.S. *Saint John*, commissioned in December 1943 at Montreal. She joined the U-boat hunting group EG 9 in time for the D-Day landings, and spent the summer of 1944 in the English Channel searching for subs. On September 1, 1944, *Saint John* and stablemate H.M.C.S. *Swansea* sank

H.M.C.S. *Caraquet*, the flagship of the 31st (Canadian) Minesweeping Flotilla. On D-Day, *Caraquet* and her sister ships cleared the approaches to Omaha beach, the site of bloody American landings. LAC PA-125863

H.M.C.S. *Saint John*, one of five River-class frigates named for
New Brunswick communities. Her score of two U-boat kills was
second only to that of frigate H.M.C.S. *Swansea*. Harold Wright

U-247 off Land's End, Cornwall, becoming the only Canadian frigates
to sink a U-boat in the summer campaign. Much of the work was done
by *Saint John*, which lingered over the suspected U-boat and pounded it
with depth charges until a large oil slick appeared. *Saint John* repeated her
success in February 1945, when, operating alone, she found and destroyed
U-309 in Moray Firth, Scotland. Her two U-boat kills made *Saint John* the
R.C.N.'s second-highest-scoring frigate of the war (*Swansea* sank four).
Run hard and badly beaten up by all the depth charges she had dropped
in shallow waters, *Saint John* was scrapped in 1947.

Four River-class frigates from the second building program also carried
New Brunswick names. *St. Stephen* was commissioned in July 1944 at
Vancouver, but by this stage, the officials in Ottawa had to be creative in
order to avoid conflict with British vessels bearing similar names. Thus,
Strathadam, commissioned in September at Vancouver, was named for

Newcastle, while *Inch Arran* and *Sussexvale*, both commissioned in November at Lauzon, Quebec, were named for Dalhousie and Sussex, respectively.

Strathadam spent her war in EG 25 hunting U-boats in British waters. On March 6, 1945, in the Irish Sea, she combined with two other frigates from her group to sink *U-1302*, *Strathadam*'s attack delivering the fatal blow. Sold from the fleet reserve in 1950, *Strathadam* served in the Israeli navy until 1959. *Sussexvale* had a very quiet war, was completely rebuilt in the 1950s as a Prestonian-class escort, and was finally scrapped in 1966. *Inch Arran*'s experience was virtually identical to that of *Sussexvale*. She had a quiet war and, after a few years in fleet reserve, was rebuilt and served for years as a Prestonian-class escort. *Inch Arran* has the distinction of being the last of the River-class frigates to serve in the R.C.N.: she went to the wreckers in 1970.

Chapter Six

Building the Modern Fleet, 1945-2003

After the Second World War, New Brunswick continued to have a close association with the Canadian navy. This was especially so for Saint John Shipbuilding and Drydock Company Ltd. Its huge dry dock provided an ideal maintenance and refit facility for the fleet, particularly for larger vessels, including the aircraft carriers *Magnificent* and *Bonaventure*. During the 1950s and 1960s, Saint John also built minesweepers and tugs for the navy, as well as the two fleet support ships *Protecteur* and *Preserver*, which remain the core of the fleet's afloat logistics in the early twenty-first century. Perhaps even more impressive was the role that Saint John played in building the combat fleet itself in the late twentieth century. As the navy celebrated its centennial in 2010, the majority of its major warships, the twelve ships of the Canadian Patrol Frigate program, had been designed and mostly constructed in a state-of-the-art facility in New Brunswick.

The key to the special role played by New Brunswick in building the modern Canadian navy was the large dry dock located at Courtney Bay in East Saint John. The dry dock was opened in 1923 under the name St. John Drydock and Shipbuilding Company, a subsidiary of Canada Dredging Co. Ltd. of Midland, Ontario. Announced in 1918, it was to be the biggest dry dock in the world with a length of 1,150 feet and a width at the bottom of 125 feet. According to the *New York Times*, "It will accommodate the largest vessel, naval or mercantile, which is now afloat or planned." The opening attracted many dignitaries, including Baron

H.M.C.S. *Magnificent* under repair in Saint John dry dock in the late 1940s. Harold Wright

The Saint John shipyard under construction 1923. Built by Canada Dredging Co. Ltd. of Ontario, it was the biggest dry dock in the world at the time. Purchased by the Irving family of New Brunswick in the 1950s, it became the birthplace of the modern Canadian navy. Gary Copeland

Byng of Vimy, Canada's governor-general. The company was purchased by K.C. Irving in the 1950s and renamed Saint John Shipbuilding and Dry Dock Co., Ltd. By the 1980s, it would become known as Saint John Shipbuilding Limited (S.J.S.L.) and was the key facility of the Irving Shipbuilding group.

In the post-war period, the Royal Canadian Navy underwent an enormous expansion based on a new class of Canadian-designed anti-submarine destroyer escort known as the St. Laurent class. Eventually, twenty-four St. Laurents and their derivatives were built, forming the core of the fleet until the 1990s. Sleek, powerful, and modern, the St. Laurents were built at shipyards in British Columbia, Quebec, and Nova Scotia, where the federal government intended to maintain construction capacity. As part of the fleet expansion, however, the R.C.N. needed minesweepers and tugs, and contracts for twenty 390-foot-long minesweepers eventually were let, and two of these modest projects were awarded to Saint John. H.M.C.S. *Fundy*, the second to bear that name, was commissioned on March 19, 1954, followed on July 10 by the second H.M.C.S. *Miramichi*. *Fundy* served with the fleet on the west coast until the 1990s, when the old minesweepers of the Training Squadron were replaced by new Maritime Coastal Defence Vessels. *Miramichi* lasted only a few days in R.C.N. service before she and five other Bay-class vessels were transferred to the French Navy in 1954. She was replaced by a third H.M.C.S. *Miramichi*, built in British Columbia.

Although New Brunswick was shut out of the massive St. Laurent project, changes in the operational environment at sea soon provided Saint John with a chance to contribute major vessels to the fleet. By the late 1950s, submarines had begun to carry nuclear-tipped missiles, and it became necessary to track Soviet subs carrying these deadly cargoes throughout their passage of the North Atlantic. The St. Laurent-class destroyer escorts would have to be modified to carry the shipboard helicopters needed for this mission. However, the real limitation on the fleet's ability to do its job in the North Atlantic was the requirement to return to port to refuel. If the fleet could carry its own fuel, it could virtually double its operational capability. And so the R.C.N. went shopping for "Auxiliary Oiler, Replenishment" (A.O.R.) ships.

The first contract went to Davies Shipyard in Lauzon, Quebec, where H.M.C.S. *Provider* was laid down in 1961. At 22,700 tons fully loaded and just over 550 feet long, *Provider* was the largest warship ever built in Canada for the R.C.N. Some 12,000 tons of that weight consisted of fuel, diesel oil, and aviation gas for the fleet. She entered service in September 1963, and her impact on the fleet's capability was tremendous from the outset. But the design was not ideal, and lessons were learned. Moreover, even "gas stations" need maintenance and leave for their crews, and one A.O.R. was not going to be enough. In 1966, the navy awarded contracts for two more improved A.O.R.s.

It is entirely likely that the politics of shipbuilding played a major role in Saint John's initial foray into major construction for the navy. In 1966 S.J.S.L. lost out in the bidding on the contract for a major refit of the carrier *Bonaventure*. That refit, with its cost overruns, ultimately cost the navy its only aircraft carrier—it is interesting to speculate on what might have happened to Canadian naval aviation had the contract gone to New Brunswick. In compensation, however, S.J.S.L. was awarded a contract worth $47.5 million to build two new A.O.R.s. The contract, then the largest ever placed with a Canadian shipyard, brought needed employment opportunities to the shipyard and Saint John region, guaranteeing work into the 1970s. Then-premier Louis J. Robichaud hailed the decision, indicating it would have "an enormous impact on the economy of Saint John, and indeed, of the entire province." The editor of *The Telegraph-Journal* called it a tribute to the recognized skill of the workforce and management of the dry dock. Construction began in spring 1967 and was completed within three years. The yard employed approximately three thousand workers at peak production periods during the construction.

The contract also came during a period of change in the shipbuilding industry in Canada. The workforce, the technology employed in the construction process, and the styles of management that supervised it all were significantly altered. The traditional "craft" type of approach to ship construction gave way to an assembly process whereby the ships were produced on a unit principle. The plan of construction was controlled using a "critical path" method: all the necessary elements—engine outfitting, maintenance, painting, fabrication—were incorporated into an overall guiding plan that ensured components or units were ready when required for the next stage of construction. All this ensured that Saint John would meet the contract delivery date. Cutting steel into the required shapes and their assembly into units were carried out simultaneously for both vessels. The workforce waxed and waned depending on the volume of work, but it was made up of increasingly skilled tradesmen organized under several unions. The traditional rigid hierarchical approach to management gave way to management by objectives. The new approaches took time to work out, and the project experienced several delays due to labour-management issues—when *Preserver* was commissioned in 1970, tension was still apparent. But, as company president K.C. Irving stated, "I would remind both management and labour that a better system—a better working relationship—must be found if we are to be successful in the future." Labour relations—a challenge to all shipyards in a rapidly changing and highly competitive industry—would continue to be problematic in Saint John right through the Canadian Patrol Frigate program two decades later.

The keels of both vessels were laid on October 17, 1967. *Protecteur* was launched July 18, 1968, and commissioned on August 30, 1969. *Preserver*'s launch followed almost a year later, on May 29, 1969, and she was commissioned on August 7, 1970. In a tribute to the quality of the work done in the Saint John yard, General J.V. Allard, chief of defence, stated at *Protecteur*'s commissioning, "This ship is as well constructed as any I have ever seen and we'll certainly be proud to show her to anyone in the world." With these two new ships, a new dimension opened in the navy's capacity to protect Canada's sovereignty and assist in Western efforts to counter increasing Soviet naval presence around the world. And, as things turned out, General Allard's compliment to S.J.S.L. was well founded. Both A.O.R.s were indeed built extremely well; forty years later, they are still in service and remain the key to the fleet's global deployability.

Both *Protecteur* and *Preserver* have a standard displacement of approximately 8,380 tons, increasing to 24,500 tons when fully loaded. Their overall

The fleet support ships H.M.C.S. *Protecteur* (number 509)
and H.M.C.S. *Preserver* near completion in Saint John in 1970:
the beginning of more than four decades of stellar service. Gary Copeland

length is 564 feet 4 inches with beam of 75 feet 6 inches and a draught of 32
feet 10 inches. They are powered by General Electric steam turbine engines
supplied by two Babcock and Wilcox boilers giving a top speed of twenty
knots — all driven by a single propeller. They carry enough fuel and stores
to provision a group of six destroyers for six weeks. They are capable of
holding and replenishing at sea liquid cargo, including fresh water, diesel,
and aviation fuel. They also supplement the medical and dental facilities
of destroyers and frigates. While obviously not intended for direct combat,
they were armed from the outset, primarily for self-defence, with one twin
3-inch gun mounting on the bow. By the early twenty-first century, they
had also been fitted with two 20mm Phalanx close-in weapons systems
capable of firing 4,500 rounds a minute and six .50-calibre machine guns.
They also carry three CH-124 Sea King helicopters.

Although built to provide fuel and stores to the fleet, *Protecteur* and
Preserver have proven remarkably versatile ships. Much of their first two
decades of operational service was limited to the North Atlantic and
North Pacific, but as the Canadian navy began to deploy to more distant
waters in the post-Cold War era, the A.O.R.s were crucial in support of
those efforts. *Protecteur* was among the contingent of ships sent to the
Persian Gulf in 1991 as part of Operation *Desert Shield* and later Operation
Friction. Upon her return in 1992, she was assigned to the Pacific Fleet

and underwent a major refit in 1993-1994. *Protecteur* was again active in foreign operations in 1999, when she was deployed off the coast of East Timor as part of an Australian-led multinational force to quell a civil war and provide peacekeeping. *Protecteur*'s mission was to bring fuel and supplies to the land forces, and her supply department also was responsible for coordinating all supplies and personnel coming into the theatre by sea. Her crew also assisted the Timorese in rebuilding around the capital. Meanwhile, *Preserver* and her crew were vital to the sustainability of Canada's UN mission to Somalia during Operation *Deliverance*, provided humanitarian aid to Florida residents in the aftermath of Hurricane Andrew, and assisted in the recovery effort following the crash of Swissair Flight 111 off Peggys Cove, Nova Scotia, in 1998.

Despite recent announcements indicating the government's intention to build new supply ships, the Saint John A.O.R.s will steam on well into the twenty-first century. Although Irving Shipbuilding won a $44.7 million contract to refit *Preserver* and keep her going for years to come, the work, begun in April 2010, will be done by Irving's new shipbuilding and repair firms in Halifax.

By the mid-1970s, the first Cold War fleet of St. Laurent-class destroyer escorts needed to be replaced. Their steam engines were no longer responsive enough for the age of high-speed, sea-skimming missiles. Only the new Tribal-class destroyers, recently completed in Quebec yards, had the necessary combination of cruising diesels and gas turbine engines needed for quick sprints to compete in the new tactical and operational environment. The navy also needed bigger, faster, longer-ranged ship-borne helicopters to tackle missile-firing submarines at safer distances. At the strategic level, NATO was also being pressured to modernize its

H.M.C.S. *Preserver* at New York during Fleet Week, 2009. Photo by US Navy Mass Communication Specialist Petty Officer 2nd Class Erica R. Gardner.
DND Photo

conventional forces to reduce its reliance on nuclear weapons to deter aggression by the Warsaw Pact.

The navy managed to sell the project to the federal cabinet on its industrial benefits, and the project to build a new combat fleet began in 1977 with the definition of detailed program requirements and the call for submissions from industry on their proposed approaches. The final "Project Requirement and Statement of Work" was issued in 1978, and preliminary bids were received in December. The navy spent the next few years tailoring its requirements in an attempt to optimize capability, size, and cost. Part of the challenge was the anaemic state of the Canadian shipbuilding industry. The last warships it had constructed were the four DDH 280 Tribal-class destroyers launched in Quebec earlier in the decade, and *Protecteur* and *Preserver* completed at Saint John a few years before that. Apart from refits and modernizations, little work was being done in Canadian yards, and the skills and facilities needed to produce modern vessels were at a low point. While foreign designs and foreign-built ships could be put into service more quickly, political considerations demanded a "made in Canada" fleet.

In 1980, two of the original five bidders for the new frigates were selected to submit final proposals. Given the size of the contract, the highly political nature of its implications, and the perilous state of Canadian shipbuilding, the Trudeau Liberal government made it perfectly clear that the award would go to the contractor with the best bid. Moreover, that decision would be made by the appropriate federal government agencies, such as Public Works and Treasury Board, without political interference.

The two final consortia bidding on what was now called the Canadian Patrol Frigate (C.P.F.) program were SCAN Marine Incorporated of Montreal (a Pratt & Whitney Canadian subsidiary) and S.J.S.L. of Saint John. They were to "draw up a proposal for the ship design, construction plans, management plans, software and support plans for the implementation of the project. At the same time they were to establish definitive costs of their proposals." Their final proposals, which together weighed some nine tons — S.J.S.L.'s technical documents alone amounted to 38,378 pages — were delivered in October 1982. The difference between the SCAN Marine bid and that of S.J.S.L. was $1 billion — about twenty-five percent of the total estimated program cost. When S.J.S.L.'s bid was revealed, SCAN adjusted its own to match. The Treasury Board, however, dismissed that company's revised bid — in view of the enormity of the project, the years of design and calculation, and the mountain of supporting documentation in the bidding process, SCAN's readjustment seemed cavalier — and, in early 1983, awarded the contract to S.J.S.L.

The decision to award the contract to New Brunswick exploded in the federal cabinet like a bomb. Shipbuilding in Canada could never be a non-partisan activity: Trudeau's Quebec caucus threatened to defect, which would have brought down the government. The navy, however, stepped in with a clever solution. It had been trying to obtain $500 million to modernize its four Tribal-class destroyers, and now it proposed that, if S.J.S.L. was to be the lead yard for the C.P.F., then subcontracting three of the six new ships to Quebec shipyards along with the Tribal modernization, would make the value of federal spending on ships in Quebec and New Brunswick about equal. The cabinet bought the plan.

Accordingly, with S.J.S.L. as the lead yard on the project, Montreal's PARAMAX became the lead subcontractor for combat system integration. PARAMAX was a new Canadian company established by the Sperry Corporation, which, consistent with the goal of the project's industrial benefits accruing to Canada, committed to making the company Canadian-controlled by the end of the project. Overall design and project management would rest with S.J.S.L., which would also build three of the ships; the other three would be constructed in Quebec, two by Marine Industries Ltd. in Quebec City and the other by Versatile Corp. in Lauzon.

With a price tag of $3.85 billion, the C.P.F. program was the largest procurement contact in Canadian military history. S.J.S.L. was responsible for the total system integration from design to trials. The intent was to hand fully operational ships over to the navy at completion. The project required hundreds of skilled professionals from a myriad disciplines, not the least of which was effective project management. The design was state of the art, and quality assurance, inbound logistics, and manufacturing techniques all had to be upgraded to match. This also resulted in a significant increase

Aerial view of the Saint John shipyard during the Canadian Patrol Frigate program: four frigates are seen lying alongside. The large building on the right is where the mega-modules were assembled. Gary Copeland

in the skills of the Saint John and area labour force, which would benefit future construction projects outside the shipbuilding industry. At its peak, 2,300 hourly paid workers and 3,300 S.J.S.L. employees worked on the project. The Saint John facility was extensively upgraded, with approximately $350 million spent in developing infrastructure. Over seven hundred Canadian companies, including many local firms, supplied either expertise or materials to the frigate project. The expertise gained would transfer quickly to other parts of the Saint John economy.

The upgrade to the Saint John facility and Irving's acquisition of several other Maritime shipyards allowed an advanced modular approach to frigate construction. Each vessel was built from some 250,000 precisely cut pieces of steel plate using computer-assisted plasma cutters. The ships also included eighty kilometres of T-bars and stiffeners to support the steel plate. These became the building blocks of "mega-modules." Some nine stories high and weighing from 140 to 450 tons, these were largely completed indoors — a significant contribution to efficiency. Each frigate was assembled using nine mega-modules, and by the time they were fitted together in the graving dock, over ninety percent of the insulation was done along with some flooring. The modular system allowed for multiple vessels to be worked on without causing disruptions — another dramatic time saver. By the time a frigate was completed it included 2,500 tons of steel, more than one million fasteners, thirty-five kilometres of pipe, 206 kilometres of welding, and 213 kilometres of electrical wiring. The paint alone on each vessel was worth $1 million.

The shipyard also became more efficient as managers and workers became more familiar with the modular system. The first ship of the class, H.M.C.S. *Halifax*, took five million person-hours of work. The finished product was a state-of-the-art warship displacing 4,750 tons. She had better stability and sea-keeping characteristics than the class of vessels she was replacing, as well as a reduced radar cross-section to that of a small fishing vessel (making her better able to reflect radar waves and produce a smaller signature on a radar screen). Her sensor system could detect submarines at ranges of 150 miles or more, and would be even more effective in conjunction with the modern helicopters—the EH 101—that were then on order.

Halifax was powered by two gas turbine engines driving variable pitch propellers that gave her a tactical manoeuvring speed of more than twenty-seven knots and an ability to sprint quickly to avoid missiles. Economical cruising was achieved through a twenty-cylinder diesel engine. All equipment and systems, including the engines, were shock mounted to reduce noise signatures through the hull and in the water. Her command, control, and communications layout and suite were the best in their class in the world.

Halifax's offensive and defensive systems were no less impressive. She carried MK 46 torpedoes capable of being launched by ship or helicopter, as well as sixteen vertically launched Sea Sparrow surface-to-air missiles and eight Harpoon surface-to-surface missiles with a range of eighty miles. On the forecastle was mounted a Bofors 57mm MK2 gun capable of delivering 220 rounds per minute of automatic fire, and a Phalanx MK 15 CIWS that delivered 3,000 rounds per minute. In addition, the vessel carried a full suite of electronic countermeasures.

Between the award and the actual start of construction in 1987, when the keel plates for *Halifax* were laid, S.J.S.L. put together the final plans for the project. By early 1985, problems became apparent, and delays were now expected. S.J.S.L. went through a significant management shakeup with the retirement of the shipyard's president, the appointment of a new manager of the C.P.F. project, and the reassignment of some senior executives. Meetings were held with the federal defence minister regarding "expected but unspecified delays in the program." Problems with finalizing the ships' design and forecasting workloads were the chief culprits in pushing back the start date of *Halifax* by at least nine months.

In addition to problems with the design phase, S.J.S.L. encountered labour difficulties that threatened to affect delivery schedules. The yard's workforce of about 1,200 had been unemployed for more than a year, so the frigate program was welcome news. Less pleasant, however, was management's insistence on more trade flexibility among the five unions representing the workforce. The unions also objected to S.J.S.L.'s decision to adopt modular construction techniques, rather than the conventional method of shipbuilding in dry dock that the unions favoured. Negotiations intended to reach a new collective agreement that would allow S.J.S.L. to move forward on the project and keep costs within the ceiling specified by the Department of National Defence were at a standstill, with the Marine Workers (the largest of the five unions) refusing to discuss the issue. Similar labour relations issues were being experienced by the shipyards in Quebec.

The Saint John yard continued to experience problems into 1986. By then, *Halifax* was expected to be delivered six months late and the scheduled delivery of the next ship, H.M.C.S. *Vancouver*, was now set at September 1990—five months behind schedule. The project experienced another delay when steel plates for *Halifax*'s hull had to be returned due to pitting; the replacement steel took four weeks to arrive. By this stage, the Mulroney Progressive Conservative government had approved funding for Batch II of the C.P.F. program, and the stakes were high. S.J.S.L. lost no time in submitting its proposal: the ship design would remain the same but would allow for new equipment to ensure the latest technology was on board. But the company would have to resolve its problems if it was to secure the new contract.

In early 1987, another threat to S.J.S.L.'s bid for Batch II emerged. Its original competitor, and now subcontractor of three ships of the first contract, Marine Industries Ltd (M.I.L.) was poised to take over the ailing Quebec shipbuilder Versatile Corp., pending resolution of specific labour issues. This would give M.I.L. significant economies of scale and technical depth. Moreover, major portions of the funds to purchase Versatile were coming from the federal and Quebec governments, with the former kicking in $35 million and the latter providing $53 million toward yard modernization and another $40 million in loan guarantees. The head of Ontario's biggest shipbuilder, Canadian Shipbuilding and Engineering Ltd., summed up the feelings of most of the shipbuilding industry in Canada: "I regard these grants as frightening. It's unfair competition." In addition, M.I.L. now was building all three new frigates earmarked for

Fitting the bow module of H.M.C.S. *Fredericton*.

Corporal Peter Reed

Quebec (the original three had been split between M.I.L. and Versatile). With the second group of six frigates yet to be awarded, opinion was divided as to which yard would become the prime contractor.

From S.J.S.L.'s point of view, it must have been somewhat reassuring that, by fall 1987, its yard was already cutting steel for the second frigate and rapidly gaining expertise unavailable to its competitors. By the end of September, *Halifax* was about one-third complete and was expected to conduct sea trials by October 1989, with *Vancouver* still being scheduled for handover to the navy in September 1990. There were 950 hourly employees working at the Saint John yard, a number that was expected to rise to 1,200 by the end of the year. An almost equal number of white-collar workers were similarly employed in design and management, attesting to the complexity of the job. The usual ratio on civilian vessel construction was ten workers on the shop floor to every white-collar worker.

By October 1987, the fight for Batch II was heating up. Ottawa had asked S.J.S.L. to revise its proposal to include building two of the frigates in Quebec. S.J.S.L. estimated that lost efficiencies would drive project costs up by $200 million, a claim refuted by M.I.L. executives. Quebec industry minister Daniel Johnson went on record as saying that, despite the increased cost, the contract should be shared: "There's enough work to go around." S.J.S.L. then warned that the additional cost of splitting construction between New Brunswick and Quebec had risen to an estimated $80 million per ship. The delay of a cabinet decision into 1988 was also a problem, as subcontractors' commitments under the original proposal would expire on January 1, 1988, and project costs would escalate again, since the new bids that would have to be acquired likely would reflect increases due to inflation.

The federal government was sympathetic to S.J.S.L.'s case and, by the end of November, it had been leaked that S.J.S.L. would be the prime contractor on Batch II. The only question under discussion was how many of the six would be built in Quebec. The political discussion was becoming even more complicated as M.I.L. and S.J.S.L. were also jockeying for position on the navy's $7-8 billion nuclear submarine contract and the Mulroney government was looking for support for the Meech Lake Accord. In the midst of this, a good portion of the federal cabinet and the defence department were insisting that all six new frigates should go to S.J.S.L. — to most, the extra costs associated with splitting the contract were unpalatable.

M.I.L. and its supporters in government remained adamant that some portion of Batch II should go to Quebec, predicting shipyard closures and massive layoffs if at least two new frigates were not built there — M.I.L. had no work scheduled beyond 1991, when the third frigate of the first contract was scheduled to be completed. All the posturing came to naught: on December 18, Ottawa awarded the contract to S.J.S.L., with no requirement that any of the ships be built outside New Brunswick. With that decision, S.J.S.L. became the prime contractor for the combat fleet on which the navy would rely at the start of the new millennium.

The C.P.F. project had a dramatic effect on Saint John and, by extension, the whole province. By the end of 1988, hundreds of millions of dollars had been pumped into the local economy. Moreover, S.J.S.L. had been transformed into a world-class operation employing more than four thousand people. A new entrepreneurial class was developing that could lead to new ventures, as skills and technology were leveraged in a new phase of diversification, something sorely needed in the Maritimes. The second batch of ships ensured work for the next six to eight years, with all of the associated benefits to the region. Saint John was once again becoming a centre of excellence for naval ship construction.

With *Halifax* floating in the dry dock by late 1988 and getting its finishing touches before sea trials, *Vancouver* well on its way, the modules for *Toronto* well advanced, and the contract for Batch II in hand, things were going well for S.J.S.L. But completing the project would never have been a matter of smooth sailing. M.I.L.'s first frigate was only twenty percent complete, and tension was rising between the two shipbuilding rivals. Both were keenly eyeing the submarine contract (both included black submarines in shipyard scale models for visitors to see) and a dispute over a subcontract on the frigate program was fuelling the fire. S.J.S.L. had cut off a contract to M.I.L. Systems Engineering, which was to do part of the C.P.F. design, for non-performance, an action that quickly invited a $17 million lawsuit by M.I.L. For its part, M.I.L. claimed that there had also been delays in S.J.S.L.'s providing the required design drawings and materials. M.I.L. president Donald Challinor stated, "I've noticed a hardening of the relationship," and a report indicated there were "communications and delivery problems between the two companies." The situation in Quebec was perhaps even more charged by the cancellation of the nuclear submarine proposal in April 1989.

Delays continued to plague the project's first vessels. *Halifax*'s handover to the navy was pushed back to spring 1990. S.J.S.L. was also having problems with PARAMAX, the chief supplier and designer of the ships' weapons systems. Missed delivery dates in 1987 by the Montreal-based company had almost led to a lawsuit, and problems were being encountered with the Phalanx gun amid questions raised about its effectiveness. Concerns were also being voiced over the frigates' stability and additional weight, which the navy strongly rejected. It is reflective of the problems of large-scale contracting in Canada that Public Works arranged to have the first gearboxes for the ships' drive system shipped by the lowest bidder—a company that just happened to be from a Warsaw Pact country. These were state-of-the-art, highly sophisticated pieces of equipment, and no one—except perhaps for the civil servants in Ottawa who arranged the shipping—was surprised to learn that the crates carrying the gearboxes had been opened.

Despite the challenges, delays, and contractual wrangling, the frigate program had contributed to an economic upturn in Saint John. By the end of 1989, the shipyard was directly employing 3,200 workers, 2,000 of whom were hourly. Some five thousand additional jobs were estimated to have been created indirectly, and some $250 million in new economic activity had been spun off the project. Such had been the magnitude of the economic impact, however, that many began to be concerned about what would happen when the program ended. New contracts in shipbuilding were rare, and few were planned into the 1990s. A third batch of frigates had already been scrapped in favour of the (now also scrapped) nuclear submarine program, and many wondered what would happen to the new talents that were being developed in the region.

Economic optimism was further dampened in mid-1990 with the filing for bankruptcy of Leigh Instruments, the subcontractor responsible for developing and producing the frigates' shipboard communications systems. Already two years behind schedule and $50 million over budget, the subcontract had to be turned over to a new firm. Other delays led S.J.S.L. to file a $1.7 billion lawsuit against its competitor and major subcontractor M.I.L. for being two years behind schedule and $260 million over budget (the federal and Quebec governments eventually would come up with a $363 million aid package for M.I.L.). In the midst of this, in early August 1990, H.M.C.S. *Halifax* slipped out to sea to begin her trials, which were successfully completed by the end of the month.

With the lead ship in the class now completed, the sister ships began to roll out regularly as the dry dock improved its processes, learned how to better manage the modular construction method, and generally got better at its job. As S.J.S.L. moved on to Batch II, subcontractor issues were largely cleared up: all six ships of the second contract would be built in Saint John, eliminating one major subcontractor, and PARAMAX's weapons systems, once delivered, were proven in the first batch. *Vancouver* and *Toronto*, the last of Batch I, were completed in 1993. Of the ships in

Batch II, *Montréal* and *Fredericton* put to sea in 1994, with *Winnipeg* and *Charlottetown* following in 1995. The final two, *St. John's* and *Ottawa*, were completed in 1996. Although *Halifax* was delivered eighteen months behind schedule, *Ottawa* was finished early. By the start of 1997, Canada had some of the most modern vessels anywhere in the world, as well as some of the most up-to-date technology, which, according to one officer, "sparked more than a trace of envy in navies around the world."

Canada's final warship building program of the twentieth century, the twelve "Maritime Coastal Defence Vessels" (M.C.D.V.s), was awarded in 1992 to a consortium led by Fenco Engineering, a division of SNC-Lavalin. All were built by Halifax-Dartmouth Industries, which was purchased by Irving Shipbuilding in the 1990s, and one was commissioned H.M.C.S. *Moncton*, the second ship to carry that name. The Saint John yard, despite valiant attempts to secure new naval contracts, both domestic and foreign, met with little success in the post-C.P.F. period. By 2000, after the completion of the last frigate and two container ships, the workforce shrank to six hundred. With no further work on the horizon to take advantage of the superior skills that had developed over the C.P.F. program, the owners had few options. In 2003, with the yard having been idle for three years and in the absence of a national shipbuilding policy, the decision was made to close. The remaining employees were laid off and the search began for alternate uses for the facility. An important era in New Brunswick naval shipbuilding had come to an end.

In the 1980s, the navy reverted to naming its ships after Canadian communities. New Brunswick was honoured with two, one of which is the Maritime Coastal Defence Vessel H.M.C.S. *Moncton*. DND Photo

Conclusion

On May 4, 2010

On May ·4, 2010, the centennial anniversary of the founding of the Canadian naval service, H.M.C.S. *Fredericton* sailed into Halifax harbour. The timing was deliberate. *Fredericton* had just completed a six-month deployment to the Arabian Sea, Gulf of Aden, and Strait of Hormuz. There, in waters now familiar to Canada's sailors, *Fredericton* had chased pirates and terrorists in the sweltering tropic heat.

Operation *Saiph*, as *Fredericton*'s deployment was called, involved working with a "coalition of the willing" to check the chaos that threatened the free and peaceful movement of commerce on the waters of the Middle East. Her mission actually involved two separate activities. In the northern waters of the Arabian Gulf, along the Pakistani coast, and in through the Strait of Hormuz, the target was the flow of terrorists and the drugs that funded their campaigns. These were, in the words of Lieutenant (N) Dave Becerra, *Fredericton*'s intelligence officer, "intelligence driven" operations. The ship was linked to a global network of police, military, and special intelligence systems that targeted the movement of people, suspected terrorists, and drugs. It helped that most countries in the area are cooperating in the battle against the illegal drug trade, so laws on trafficking in hashish or cocaine were easy to enforce. A suspect vessel would be located by *Fredericton*'s helicopter and ordered to stop, and a boarding party sent over in the frigate's rigid high-speed inflatable boat (R.H.I.B.) to conduct a search.

Chasing pirates off the Somali coast and in the Gulf of Aden was a combination of patrols and "incident"-driven operations. Trade passing through the area was sometimes escorted, especially World Food Aid vessels carrying supplies to Somalia, and convoys were conducted in the Gulf of Aden. Otherwise, *Fredericton* was on the lookout for trouble. The helicopter would be airborne just before dawn for a sweep around the area to upgrade and augment the frigate's "situational awareness" following a night of steaming. The helo then would do another patrol around midday, and one at last light—when pirates preferred to attack.

The pirates *Fredericton* was looking for bear little resemblance to the garishly dressed swashbucklers of Hollywood movies. Somali pirates—and they are invariably Somali—are generally poor young men driven onto the sea by the chaos of their country. Equipped by land-based pirate cartels, they patrol several hundred kilometres to seaward in open wooden boats propelled by powerful outboard engines. Their equipment is rudimentary: a few assault rifles, some rocket-propelled grenades, and a ladder. The boats carry basic supplies of fuel and water, and probably a supply of *khat*, a local leaf they chew for its narcotic effect.

These small pirate boats generally operate in pairs and attack ships from the stern, approaching on either quarter so that, whether the ship steers left or right, one boat is well placed to lay alongside. If all goes well, the pirates are on board in a few minutes and the crew succumbs without a fight. The ship is then taken into port and the ransom process begins.

Not all pirate ventures end well, and *Fredericton*'s crew heard tales of small boats found well out into the Indian Ocean with desiccated bodies aboard: the result of engine failure or the pirates' running out of water. In some instances, the crews of merchant ships, or the security personnel they have hired, fight back.

Fredericton's anti-piracy and anti-terrorist patrols were largely uneventful. For six months, she shifted from the Strait of Hormuz to the Strait of Bab-el-Mendeb between the Gulf of Aden and the Red Sea. "The action always seemed to be elsewhere," Lieutenant Commander Steve Waddell, *Fredericton*'s captain, observed. "When we were in a quiet sector, things would flare up somewhere else. By the time we got to the scene

At the time of the Canadian naval centennial in 2010, most of the fleet was designed and built in New Brunswick, including H.M.C.S. *Fredericton*, the only major Canadian warship to be deployed overseas that year. She is seen here in the Mediterranean returning from her six-month deployment to the Arabian Sea and Indian Ocean. Milner Collection.

of the action things were quiet again, but then something would happen in the area we just left." It seems that *Fredericton*'s reputation as a "lucky ship," inherited from her predecessor, the Second World War corvette that never saw a shot fired in anger, has survived.

But the crew, the helicopter, and the ship performed superbly. *Fredericton* did everything Waddell asked of her and under conditions for which she was never designed. The C.P.F.s had been intended for use in the North Atlantic, so one of the greatest challenges in the Arabian Gulf was keeping the ship and its crew cool. The ship's four air-conditioning systems — "chillers" in naval parlance — were mission-critical systems. In theory, Canadian Patrol Frigates have one hundred percent redundancy in their allocation of chillers: in the North Atlantic only two are usually needed, primarily to keep the computer, combat, and sensor systems cool, while the engines can be cooled with seawater. But when the sea temperature is over 30 degrees Celsius and the air temperature is at nearly

50 degrees, the four chillers work continuously. Had even one of them failed, *Fredericton* would have had to scurry into port for repairs. None did. *Fredericton*'s aging Sea King helicopters also performed exceptionally well, typically flying six or eight hours per day. When her first helicopter reached the limits of its allowable flying time, it was switched for another during a long layover in Dubai. The second worked flawlessly, too, nursed by a skilled collection of maintainers in *Fredericton*'s helicopter detachment. But the flying was hard on the aircrew, who had to operate the helicopter without either air conditioning or cooled flying suits. By the time the deployment was over, *Fredericton*'s helicopter had flown more than 650 hours, a new record for helicopters deployed to the Middle East.

When *Fredericton* turned for home in early April 2010, Operation *Saiph* had gone off without a hitch. The crew's reward was a few days in Egypt and a chance to see the pyramids, a long weekend in Istanbul, and a quiet cruise across the Mediterranean. Some departments within the ship used the time to train personnel, while engine trials tested propulsion in anticipation of a prolonged docking starting in 2011, and the helicopter continued to fly.

Temperatures went down and the seas rose as *Fredericton* travelled west. Passage through the Strait of Gibraltar under low heavy clouds, cool temperatures, and rain brought smiles to many faces on board: *Fredericton* had not seen rain since before Christmas. Chief Petty Officer Gerry Ross would have liked the rain a little earlier. As the ship's "Buffer," the petty officer responsible for topside appearance, he had already spent some time hosing off the dust that had accumulated on the ship during long days at sea off the Arabian Peninsula. Once out into the Atlantic, where the sea colour turned deep green and the long ocean swell caused the frigate to pitch and roll, her crew began to feel that they were "home." Close enough, at least, to commit the ashes of several deceased veteran sailors to the deep at the request of their relatives. As Coxswain Percy Rasmussen said, "We couldn't bury them in a foreign sea."

The meander home included a weekend in Madeira for a "run ashore." Not only did Madeira, known for its wine, prove to be a semi-tropical paradise, but also a place where, for the first time in six months, the ship

H.M.C.S. *Brunswicker*, the current naval establishment in Saint John and the last official navy presence in the province.
DND Photo

was able to stand down from the high level of security she had maintained since November. The .50 calibre machine guns on the quarterdeck and the bridge wings used to protect the ship from suicide craft were quietly stowed. So, too, were the assault rifles and pistols of the duty watch, so much in evidence during her port visits in the Middle East. And the crew could straggle ashore and enjoy the island without fear of kidnapping or worse.

Then, a slow — much too slow for many aboard — passage to St. John's, Newfoundland, on the frigate's diesel engines followed in late April and early May. The long days of heat and a flat calm were now replaced by a six-metre following sea that set *Fredericton* into a rhythm familiar to North Atlantic veterans. In Newfoundland, a few local sailors were allowed to leave the ship, making room for family and dignitaries for the final passage to Halifax.

Finally, on the morning of May 4, 2010, *Fredericton* motored quietly up Halifax harbour to a tumultuous welcome from friends, family, the local community, and the national media. All eyes were on the navy and on Halifax, and rightfully so. That the ship was named for New Brunswick's capital city drew little, if any, comment. In fairness, that was not remarkable: all of the modern warships in the Canadian navy are named for communities. It might just as well have been *Charlottetown* or *Vancouver* or *Toronto* arriving.

But it bears repeating that those vessels — like most of the operational fleet in the year of Canada's naval centennial and like Canada's National Naval Memorial itself, H.M.C.S. *Sackville* — were built in New Brunswick. It serves to remind us that, for the past four hundred years, New Brunswick has played a crucial but often neglected role in Canada's naval history.

Acknowledgements

As with all books this is the work of many hands, and we have drawn our information from a great variety of sources. Thanks to Faye Kert, Roger Sarty, and Doug Knight for the pioneering research they produced for their books in the New Brunswick Military Heritage Project series, upon which we have shamelessly built. Thanks also to Louis-Philippe Campeaux at the Directorate of History and Heritage, National Defence Headquarters, for material on Saint John, including photos of its fleet; to Chantal Leblanc of the *Lieu historique national du Canada de la Bataille-de-la-Ristigouche* for the photos of Fred Werthman's wonderful model of *Le Machault*; to Michel Boudreau, president of the *Société historique Machault*, for sharing that society's illustrations of the Battle of the Restigouche; to Armand Robichaud for sharing his research on Acadian privateers; to Harold Wright of Saint John for sharing his illustrations; to Josh Smith of the US Merchant Marine Academy for sharing his work on privateering in the War of 1812 (which will appear in due course in this series); to Gary Copeland for sharing his experience at Saint John Shipbuilding and for the use of some of his photos; to Doug Knight for ordering photos for us; and to Janet Bishop of the New Brunswick Museum. Thanks also go out to the staff at the Provincial Archives of New Brunswick and the University of New Brunswick Archives. As in the past, thanks to Mike Bechthold for his wonderful maps, to Brent Wilson, Barry Norris, and Megan Woodworth for their editing, to Angela Williams for compiling the index, and to Julie Scriver and Jaye Haworth for their superb design work. We would like to extend an especial thank you to John Horton for allowing us to use his painting of H.M.C.S. *Sackville* on the cover.

Selected Bibliography

"Canada's $9-billion warships." *Financial Post Magazine*, June 1, 1994.

Department of National Defence. "Reports of Proceedings, HMCS *Captor II* (Base), Saint John NB," September 1939-December 1944, File 81/520/1000-5-11. Ottawa: Directorate of History and Heritage, National Defence Headquarters.

Hadley, Michael L. *U-Boats against Canada: German Submarines in Canadian Waters.* Montreal; Kingston, ON: McGill-Queen's University Press, 1985.

Kennedy, Tony M. "Warfare along the Disputed Acadian/Wopanahkik Frontier: A Historical Analysis of Maliseet Warfare and Diplomacy, 1600-1842." Unpublished M.A. thesis, University of New Brunswick, 2008.

Kert, Faye M. *Trimming Yankee Sails: Pirates and Privateers of New Brunswick.* Fredericton, NB: Goose Lane Editions and the New Brunswick Military Heritage Project, 2005.

Little, C.H., ed. "The Battle of the Restigouche." Occasional Paper 10. Halifax: Maritime Museum of Canada, 1962.

Milner, Marc. *Canada's Navy: The First Century.* 2nd ed. Toronto: University of Toronto Press, 2009.

Robichaud, Armand. *Les flibustiers de l'Acadie.* Lévis, QC: Les Éditions de la Francophonie, 2009.

Sarty, Roger, and Doug Knight. *Saint John Fortifications, 1630-1956.* Fredericton, NB: Goose Lane Editions and the New Brunswick Military Heritage Project, 2003.

Snider, C.N.S. *Under the Red Jack: Privateers of the Maritime Provinces in the War of 1812.* Toronto: Mason Book Company, nd.

Wells, W.R. "US Revenue Cutters Captured in the War of 1812." *American Neptune* 58 (3, 1998): 225-242.

Photo Credits

The upper front cover painting appears courtesy of the Bailey Collection, Mariner's Museum, Newport News, VA; the lower front cover painting appears courtesy of Alan Somerville, Fidelis Printmaking.The painting on page 14 by A.S. Scott appears courtesy of http://www.nelson.com/nelson/school/discovery/images/evening/pre1760/daulnay.gif. The photo on page 19 appears courtesy of Lieu historique national du Canada de la Bataille-de-la-Restigouche. The maps on pages 21 and 71 appear courtesy of Mike Bechthold. The painting on page 24 appears courtesy of La Societe historique Machault. The drawing on page 36 appears courtesy of W.W. Norton. The painting on page 47 appears courtesy of Queen's County Museum, Liverpool, N.S. (QCM). The photos on pages 54 (DND CN-1997), 72, top photo on 78, photos on pages 89, 115, 127, and 133 appear courtesy of the Department of National Defense (DND). The painting on page 57 (LAC C004078), photos on pages 87 (LAC PA-142540) and 106 (LAC PA-125863) appear courtesy of Library and Archives Canada (LAC). The photo on page 60 appears courtesy of the York-Sudbury Historical Society Museum. The photos on pages 61, 102, and 104 appear courtesy of Canadian Naval Heritage Project, Photo Archive. The photos on pages 67, 77, 81, 97, 98, 101, 103, and 131 appear courtesy of Marc Milner. The photo on page 70 appears courtesy of http://www.unithistories.com/officers/RCNVR_officers.html. The lower photo on page 78, the photos on pages 88, 107, and top photo on page 110 appear courtesy of Harold Wright. The photo on page 83 appears courtesy of www.german-uboats.com/Uboat Photos/U213.jpg. The lower photo on page 110 and photos on pages 114 and 118 appear courtesy of Gary Copeland. The photo on page 122 appears courtesy of Corporal Peter Reed. The back cover image appears courtesy of http://www.saintjohn.nbcc.nb.ca/heritage/rcn/ship_building.htm. All illustrative material is reproduced by permission.

Index

The New Brunswick Military Heritage Project

The New Brunswick Military Heritage Project, a non-profit organization devoted to public awareness of the remarkable military heritage of the province, is an initiative of the Brigadier Milton F. Gregg, VC, Centre for the Study of War and Society of the University of New Brunswick. The organization consists of museum professionals, teachers, university professors, graduate students, active and retired members of the Canadian Forces, and other historians. We welcome public involvement. People who have ideas for books or information for our database can contact us through our website: www.unb.ca/nbmhp.

One of the main activities of the New Brunswick Military Heritage Project is the publication of the New Brunswick Military Heritage Series with Goose Lane Editions. This series of books is under the direction of Marc Milner, Director of the Gregg Centre, and J. Brent Wilson, Publications Director of the Gregg Centre at the University of New Brunswick. Publication of the series is supported by a grant from the Canadian War Museum.

The New Brunswick Military Heritage Series

Volume 1

Saint John Fortifications, 1630-1956, Roger Sarty and Doug Knight

Volume 2

Hope Restored: The American Revolution and the Founding of New Brunswick, Robert L. Dallison

Volume 3

The Siege of Fort Beauséjour, 1755, Chris M. Hand

Volume 4

Riding into War: The Memoir of a Horse Transport Driver, 1916-1919, James Robert Johnston

Volume 5

The Road to Canada: The Grand Communications Route from Saint John to Quebec, W.E. (Gary) Campbell

Volume 6

Trimming Yankee Sails: Pirates and Privateers of New Brunswick, Faye Kert

Volume 7

War on the Home Front: The Farm Diaries of Daniel MacMillan, 1914-1927, ed. Bill Parenteau and Stephen Dutcher

Volume 8

Turning Back the Fenians: New Brunswick's Last Colonial Campaign,
Robert L. Dallison

Volume 9

*D-Day to Carpiquet: The North Shore Regiment and
the Liberation of Europe*, Marc Milner

Volume 10

*Hurricane Pilot: The Wartime Letters of Harry L. Gill, DFM,
1940-1943*, ed. Brent Wilson with Barbara J. Gill

Volume 11

*The Bitter Harvest of War: New Brunswick and
the Conscription Crisis of 1917*, Andrew Theobald

Volume 12

Captured Hearts: New Brunswick's War Brides,
Melynda Jarratt

Volume 13

*Bamboo Cage: The P.O.W. Diary of Flight Lieutenant Robert Wyse,
1942-1943*, ed. Jonathan F. Vance

Volume 14

*Uncle Cy's War: The First World War Letters
of Major Cyrus F. Inches*, ed. Valerie Teed

Volume 15

Agnes Warner and the Nursing Sisters of the Great War,
Shawna M. Quinn

About the Authors

Marc Milner is Director of the Brigadier Milton F. Gregg, V.C., Centre for the Study of War and Society at the University of New Brunswick. A native of Sackville, N.B., Dr. Milner earned his doctorate at the University of New Brunswick in 1983. From 1983 to 1986, Dr. Milner was a historian with the Directorate of History, Department of National Defence, Ottawa, where he wrote portions of the R.C.A.F.'s official history and the first narrative of the recent official history of the Royal Canadian Navy. He joined the History Department at U.N.B. in 1986. Since then, he has served as director of U.N.B.'s Military and Strategic Studies Programme and chair of its History Department for six years. Dr. Milner is best known for his work on naval history, including *North Atlantic Run: The Royal Canadian Navy and the Battle for the Convoys* (1985); *The U-Boat Hunters: The Royal Canadian Navy and the Offensive against Germany's Submarines* (1995); *Corvettes of the Royal Canadian Navy* (co-authored with Ken Macpherson, 1993); a novel, *Incident at North Point* (1998); a popular history, *HMCS Sackville 1940-1985* (1998, for the Canadian Naval Memorial Trust); *Battle of the Atlantic* (2003), which won the Charles P. Stacey Prize for the best book on military history in Canada for 2003-2004; and *Canada's Navy: The First Century* (1999). Dr. Milner writes a regular column on Canadian naval history for *Legion Magazine*, and the second (updated) edition of *Canada's Navy: The First Century* was published just in time for the naval centennial.

Glenn Leonard is an Assistant Professor in the University of New Brunswick's Faculty of Business Administration, where he teaches accounting, finance, and strategic management. His academic interests include accounting, business and economic history, particularly as it relates to military matters, contemporary strategic management, contemporary accounting and finance, military history (the First World War), Balkan history, terrorism, and democracy. His presentations and publications include works on the history and evolution of Canadian management theory, organization sources of professionalism, and popular perceptions of the First World War. He was awarded Professor of the Year in 2007 by the Faculty of Business Administration Undergraduate Business Society and has been a nominee for the Allan P. Stuart award for Excellence in Teaching. A long-time resident of Fredericton, he received a B.B.A. (1990) and an M.A. (2003) in History from U.N.B. and is currently completing his doctorate, also at U.N.B. He is also a professional accountant (C.A.) and has over twenty years of experience in various management positions in manufacturing, retail, wholesale, service, and non-profit organizations.